Cambridge O Level
Principles of Accounts
Workbook

Catherine Coucom

CAMBRIDGE
UNIVERSITY PRESS

University Printing House, Cambridge CB2 8BS, United Kingdom

One Liberty Plaza, 20th Floor, New York, NY 10006, USA

477 Williamstown Road, Port Melbourne, VIC 3207, Australia

4843/24, 2nd Floor, Ansari Road, Daryaganj, Delhi – 110002, India

79 Anson Road, #06–04/06, Singapore 079906

Cambridge University Press is part of the University of Cambridge.

It furthers the University's mission by disseminating knowledge in the pursuit of education, learning and research at the highest international levels of excellence.

www.cambridge.org
Information on this title: www.cambridge.org/9781107604797

© Cambridge University Press 2012

This publication is in copyright. Subject to statutory exception and to the provisions of relevant collective licensing agreements, no reproduction of any part may take place without the written permission of Cambridge University Press.

First published 2012
20 19 18 17 16 15 14 13 12 11 10 9 8 7 6 5 4 3 2

Printed in the United Kingdom by the CPI Group Ltd, Croydon CR0 4YY

A catalogue for this publication is available from the British Library

ISBN 978-1-107-60479-7 Paperback

Cambridge University Press has no responsibility for the persistence or accuracy of URLs for external or third-party internet websites referred to in this publication, and does not guarantee that any content on such websites is, or will remain, accurate or appropriate. Information regarding prices, travel timetables and other factual information given in this work are correct at the time of first printing but Cambridge University Press does not guarantee the accuracy of such information thereafter.

Contents

	Introduction	*iv*
Section 1	Preparation for the Examination	1
Section 2	Templates for the Preparation of Financial Statements	5
Section 3	Examples of Questions and Answers	15
Section 4	Short Questions on Accounting Terminology	29
Section 5	Structured Accounting Questions	32
	Appendix: Answers to Questions	99

Introduction

This workbook is intended to be used with the textbook *Cambridge O Level Principles of Accounts* (ISBN 978-1-107-60478-0) but may also be used independently. It provides additional review questions, templates of the main types of financial statements, and hints to help students prepare for the examination.

The questions are arranged in the order of the topics in the textbook. Summarised answers for most of the review questions can be found at the end of the book. The answers to questions marked with an asterisk (*) are available in the website *www.cambridgeindia.org*.

In common with most accounting textbooks, dates used in the questions throughout this book are expressed as 20-0, 20-1, 20-2 and so on.

International accounting terminology is used by large-scale companies, but it is probable that it will be used by all businesses in the near future. The O Level Principles of Accounts syllabus has moved towards applying this terminology which is now used in the O Level examination papers. It is expected that students will have knowledge of these international accounting terms. However, for a few examination sessions examiners will continue to accept answers using either new or old terminology.

Section 1

Preparation for the Examination

Many students, understandably, feel nervous or anxious about examinations. It is important to try to overcome these feelings. Thorough preparation before the examination and remaining calm once in the examination room are essential. This is no doubt much easier said than done for many students. Some practical hints included in this section, may be useful.

Devise Ways to Help Remember Things

The use of a phrase or a group of letters can be considered, that helps students to remember something. The technical name for these letters or phrases is mnemonics. Some commonly used mnemonics are given below.

1. The word "pearls" can be used as an aid to remembering the debit and credit items in a trial balance.

P E A	R L S

P = Purchases   E = Expenses   A = Assets

R = Revenue   L = Liabilities   S = Sales

2 *Cambridge O Level Principles of Accounts Workbook*

2. The words "dead clic" can also be used as an aid to remembering the debit and credit items in a trial balance.

   D Debtors (trade receivables)
   E Expenses
   A Assets
   D Drawings

   C Creditors (trade payables)
   L Liabilities
   I Income
   C Capital

3. The words "papa" and "alla" can be used as an aid to remembering the treatment of accrued and prepaid expenses and revenues in a balance sheet.

P	**Expense**	**A**
A		**L**
P	**Revenue**	**L**
A		**A**

To write this out in full it becomes:

Prepaid	**Expense**	Asset
Accrued		Liability
Prepaid	**Revenue**	Liability
Accrued		Asset

4. The word "Cocrop" can be used as an aid to remembering the errors which do not affect the balancing of a trial balance.

   C Commission
   O Omission
   C Compensating
   R Reversal
   O Original entry
   P Principle

5. Personally I like "Poor CC" (simply because it incorporates my initials!) as an aid to remembering the errors which do not affect the balancing of a trial balance.

P Principle
O Omission
O Original entry
R Reversal
C Commission
C Compensating

Many students compose their own mnemonics. Make use of anything which can help to jog the memory.

Multiple Choice Items

Many accounting examinations contain multiple choice items. These allow examiners to test candidates' knowledge over the whole of the syllabus. Some multiple choice items are purely factual, some require calculation and others require candidates to apply their knowledge to a given situation.

The following is a very general list of "dos" and "don'ts" when answering multiple choice items.

- Attempt the factual items which you feel confident about.
- Attempt the items involving a straightforward calculation.
- Attempt the items involving the application of knowledge.
- Re-read the remaining items again:
  There is often a word or phrase which provides a clue to the key.
  There are often one or two options which can be discarded as being clearly incorrect.
  If the answer is still not obvious, make an intelligent guess.
  If all else fails, select an answer at random rather than leaving an item blank.

Before the Examination

Everyone has their own way of preparing for an examination. A method which one student finds useful may not necessarily be helpful to another student. The following is a list of "dos" and "don'ts" when preparing for an examination.

- Make sure that the entire syllabus has been covered in the course of your studies.
- Make sure that you have attempted all the homework and class work assignments.
- Study your teacher's comments on your assignments.
- Ask your teacher for assistance if you are unsure about a particular topic.

- Do not rely on rote learning completely, as you must be able to apply knowledge to a variety of situations.
- Attempt as many past examination papers as possible.
- Attempt examination questions under examination conditions.
- Devise ways to help you remember things (for example, learning mnemonics)
- Plan your study time carefully.
- Do not wait until the evening before the examination to start revising.
- Make a revision plan and follow it.
- Take regular breaks from your studies, but remember that you may only have one (or two) attempts at the examination but you can socialise on many occasions after the examination.
- On the day of the examination, allow plenty of time to get to the building where the examination is to be held.

At the Examination

Again, everyone has their way of approaching an examination paper. The following is a very general list of "dos" and "don'ts" to follow inside the examination room.

- Try not to panic if the first question is on an unexpected topic.
- Read the whole of the question paper carefully.
- Read each question again before attempting an answer.
- Allocate the time according to the marks for each question.
- Start with the question which you feel most confident about.
- Do not over-run on the time per question.
- Answer the question which is being asked.
- Attempt all the questions that are required.
- Do not attempt more questions than are required – marks may not be lost but time will be.
- Generally more marks will be earned by attempting all the required questions than just completing one or two perfect answers.
- If there is an unfamiliar item within a question, do not abandon the question – complete the answer without that particular item.
- Present your answers in a tidy and orderly manner and make sure that all the words and figures are legible.
- If an answer is re-attempted, do not cross out the original answer until the new version has been completed.
- Show calculations where appropriate, as marks may be awarded even if the final answer is incorrect.
- Do not leave the examination room early – check all the answers thoroughly and attempt to complete any unfinished answers.

Section 2

Templates for the Preparation of Financial Statements

This section provides outlines of the main types of financial statements for different types of trading and non-trading organisations.

It is desirable not to learn the form of presentation by rote, but rather to understand the reasons why these accounting statements are presented in these formats. However, some students find it helpful to make use of a pro-forma accounting statement especially at the beginning of their studies.

The vertical method of presentation is used in all of the following statements.

The items shown within the accounting statements are intended to be representative of the types of items which would appear in each section – they are not intended to be definitive lists. For example, the expenses shown in the income statement may not apply to every business, and some businesses will have other types of expenses.

Similarly, the non-current assets shown in the balance sheets may not apply to every business and some businesses will have other types of non-current assets.

New terms are being used in the syllabuses to reflect the changes in terminology used in the world of business. These are given in Table 2.1. Standards which are well known and are relevant to the level of study will be used in question papers and mark schemes. Students are encouraged to use these new terms. However, for the first few years after the introduction of these terms in the syllabus, students will not be penalised for using different terms.

The templates use the traditional form of presentation, but include the new terminology where applicable.

6 *Cambridge O Level Principles of Accounts Workbook*

Table 2.1 International Standards – Terminology

International Usage	*Traditional UK Usage*
Financial statements	Final accounts
Income statement	Trading and profit and loss account
Revenue	Sales
Raw materials	Purchases
Cost of sales	Cost of goods sold
Inventory (of raw materials and finished goods)	Stock
Work in progress	Work in progress
Gross profit	Gross profit
Other operating expenses	Sundry expenses
Other operating income	Sundry income
Investment revenues	Interest receivable
Finance costs	Interest payable
Profit (before tax) for the year	Net profit
Balance sheet	Balance sheet
Non-current assets	Fixed assets
Property	Land and buildings
Plant and equipment	Plant and equipment
Investment property	Investments
Intangible assets	Goodwill etc
Current assets	Current assets
Inventory	Stock
Trade receivables	Debtors
Other receivables	Prepayments
Cash (and cash equivalents)	Bank and cash
Current liabilities	Current liabilities *Or* Creditors: amounts due within 12 months
Trade payables	Creditors
Other payables	Accruals
Bank overdrafts and loans	Loans repayable within 12 months
Non-current liabilities	Long term liabilities *Or* Creditors: amounts falling due after more than one year
Bank (and other) loans	Loans repayable after 12 months
Capital or Equity	Capital
Share capital	Share capital
Retained profits	Profit and loss account

The O level syllabus includes a table similar to that shown above.

Example 2.1

Financial statements of a trading business owned by one person:

Sole Trader
Income Statement for the year ended ....

	$	$	$
Revenue (Sales)			XXXX
Less Sales returns			XXXX
			XXXX
Less Cost of sales			
Opening inventory		XXXX	
Purchases	XXXX		
Less Purchases returns	XXXX		
	XXXX		
Less Goods for own use	XXXX		
	XXXX		
Carriage inwards	XXXX	XXXX	
		XXXX	
Less Closing inventory		XXXX	XXXX
Gross profit			XXXX
Add Other income			
Discount received			XXXX
Rent received			XXXX
Commission received			XXXX
*Profit on disposal of non-current assets			XXXX
**Reduction in provision for doubtful debts			XXXX
			XXXX
Less Expenses			
Wages and salaries		XXXX	
Office expenses		XXXX	
Rent and rates		XXXX	
Insurance		XXXX	
Office expenses		XXXX	
Motor vehicle expenses		XXXX	
Selling expenses		XXXX	
Loan interest		XXXX	
*Loss on disposal of non-current assets		XXXX	
**Provision for doubtful debts		XXXX	
Depreciation of fixtures and fittings		XXXX	
Depreciation of office equipment		XXXX	
Depreciation of motor vehicles		XXXX	XXXX
***Profit for the year			XXXX

*   If only one asset was sold during the year only one of these items will appear.
** If the provision reduces, the surplus amount is added to the gross profit; if the provision increases, the amount required is included in the expenses.
*** If the expenses exceed the gross profit plus other income, the resulting figure is described as a loss for the year.

8 *Cambridge O Level Principles of Accounts Workbook*

Sole Trader

Balance Sheet at ....

	$ Cost	$ Depreciation to date	$ Book value
Non-current assets			
Land and buildings	xxxx		xxxx
Fixtures and fittings	xxxx	xxxx	xxxx
Office equipment	xxxx	xxxx	xxxx
Motor vehicles	xxxx	xxxx	xxxx
	xxxx	xxxx	xxxx
Current assets			
Inventory		xxxx	
Trade receivables	xxxx		
Less Provision for doubtful debts	xxxx	xxxx	
Other receivables		xxxx	
Other receivables (accrued income)		xxxx	
*Bank (Cash equivalents)		xxxx	
Cash		xxxx	
		xxxx	
Current liabilities			
Trade payables	xxxx		
Other payables	xxxx		
Prepaid income	xxxx		
*Bank overdraft	xxxx	xxxx	
Net current assets			xxxx
			xxxx
Less Non-current liabilities			
Loan			xxxx
			xxxx
Financed by			
Capital			
Opening balance			xxxx
**Plus Profit for the year			xxxx
			xxxx
Less Drawings			xxxx
			xxxx

*   If the business has only one bank account, only one of these items will appear.
** If there is a loss for the year, this will be deducted rather than added.

Example 2.2

A service business is one which does not buy and sell goods. It is not necessary to prepare a trading account section of an income statement at the end of the financial year as the business does not earn a gross profit. Only a profit and loss account section of an income statement is similar to that of a trading business excluding the gross profit. The format of the balance sheet is exactly the same as that of a trading business.

Financial statements of a service business owned by one person:

Templates for the Preparation of Financial Statements 9

Sole Trader
Income Statement for the year ended ....

	$	$	$
Fees received			xxxx
Commission received			xxxx
Rent received			xxxx
Discount received			xxxx
*Profit on disposal of non-current assets			xxxx
**Reduction in provision for doubtful debts			<u>xxxx</u>
			xxxx
Less Expenses			
Wages and salaries		xxxx	
Office expenses		xxxx	
Rent and rates		xxxx	
Insurance		xxxx	
Office expenses		xxxx	
Motor vehicle expenses		xxxx	
Selling expenses		xxxx	
Loan interest		xxxx	
Bad debts		xxxx	
*Loss on disposal of non-current assets		xxxx	
**Provision for doubtful debts		xxxx	
Depreciation of fixtures and fittings		xxxx	
Depreciation of office equipment		xxxx	
Depreciation of motor vehicles		<u>xxxx</u>	<u>xxxx</u>
***Profit for the year			<u>xxxx</u>

*   * If only one asset was sold during the year only one of these items will appear.
*   ** If the provision reduces, the surplus amount is added to the gross profit; if the provision increases, the amount required is included in the expenses.
*   *** If the expenses exceed the total income, the resulting figure is described as a loss for the year.

The balance sheet of a service business of a sole trader is presented in exactly the same format as the balance sheet of a trading business of a sole trader.

Example 2.3

Financial statements of a partnership business:

The income statement of a partnership follows the same format as that of a sole trader. The only difference is that interest on a loan from a partner may be included in the expenses in the profit and loss account section of the income statement.

It is necessary to prepare an appropriation account to show the distribution of the profit for the year between the partners.

10 *Cambridge O Level Principles of Accounts Workbook*

Partnership
Profit and Loss Appropriation Account for the year ended ....

		$	$	$
Profit for the year				xxxx
Add Interest on drawings –	Partner A		xxxx	
	Partner B		xxxx	xxxx
			xxxx	
Less Interest on capital –	Partner A	xxxx		
	Partner B	xxxx	xxxx	
Partner's salary –	Partner A		xxxx	xxxx
				xxxx
*Profit shares –	Partner A		xxxx	
	Partner B		xxxx	xxxx

*Residual profit is shared in the ratio stated in the partnership agreement.

The first section of the balance sheet of a partnership follows the same format as that of a sole trader. The second section of the balance sheet has to be modified so that it shows the capital and current account of each partner.

Where the full details of the partners' current accounts are not required the "Financed by" section of a partnership balance sheet could be presented as follows:

Partnership
Extract from Balance Sheet at ....

	$ Partner A	$ Partner B	$ Total
Capital accounts	xxxx	xxxx	xxxx
*Current accounts	xxxx	xxxx	xxxx
	xxxx	xxxx	xxxx

* Where a balance is a debit balance it is shown in brackets and deducted rather than added.

Where full details of the current accounts are required the "Financed by" section of a partnership balance sheet could be presented as follows:

Partnership
Extract from Balance Sheet at ....

	$ Partner A	$ Partner B	$ Total
Capital accounts	xxxx	xxxx	xxxx
Current accounts			
*Opening balance	xxxx	xxxx	
Interest on capital	xxxx	xxxx	
Partner's salary	xxxx		
**Profit shares	xxxx	xxxx	
	xxxx	xxxx	
Less Drawings	xxxx	xxxx	
*	xxxx	xxxx	xxxx
			xxxx

* Where a balance is a debit balance, it is shown in brackets and deducted rather than added.
** Where there is a loss to share out, it is shown in brackets and deducted rather than added.

Example 2.4

Financial statements of a limited company:
The income statement of a limited company follows the same format as that of a sole trader. The only difference is that interest on debentures, preference share dividend and directors' remuneration may be included in the expenses in the income statement.

It is necessary to prepare an appropriation account to show the distribution of the net profit.

Limited Company
Profit and Loss Appropriation Account for the year ended ....

	$	$	$
Profit for the year			xxxx
Less Transfer to general reserve		xxxx	
Dividends – Ordinary paid	xxxx		
proposed	xxxx	xxxx	xxxx
Retained profit for the year			xxxx
Add Retained profit brought forward			xxxx
Retained profit carried forward			xxxx

The first section of the balance sheet of a limited company follows the same format as that of a sole trader. The second section of the balance sheet has to be modified so that it shows the share capital and reserves.

Limited Company
Extract from Balance Sheet at ....

	$
Capital and Reserves	
x% Preference shares of $x each	xxxx
Ordinary shares of $x each	xxxx
General reserve	xxxx
Retained profit	xxxx
Shareholders' funds	xxxx

Example 2.5

Financial statements of a manufacturing business:
Where a business manufactures goods it is necessary to prepare a manufacturing account to show the calculation of the cost of manufacture. This follows the same format irrespective of the ownership of the business.

12 Cambridge O Level Principles of Accounts Workbook

Sole Trader or Partnership
Manufacturing Account for the year ended ....

	$	$	$
Cost of material consumed			
Opening inventory of raw material		xxxx	
Purchases of raw material		xxxx	
Carriage on raw material		xxxx	
		xxxx	
Less Closing inventory of raw material		xxxx	xxxx
Direct wages			xxxx
Direct expenses			xxxx
Prime cost			xxxx
Add Factory overheads			
Indirect wages		xxxx	
Factory rent and rates		xxxx	
Factory insurance		xxxx	
Factory fuel and power		xxxx	
Factory general expenses		xxxx	
Depreciation of factory machinery		xxxx	xxxx
			xxxx
Add Opening work in progress			xxxx
			xxxx
Less Closing work in progress			xxxx
Production cost of goods completed			xxxx

The income statement of a manufacturing business follows the same format as that of any other form of business. The only difference is that the trading account section will include the production cost of goods completed.

Sole Trader or Partnership
Income Statement for the year ended ....

	$	$	$
Sales (Revenue)			xxxx
Less Cost of sales			
Opening inventory of finished goods		xxxx	
Production cost of goods completed		xxxx	
Purchases of finished goods		xxxx	
		xxxx	
Less Closing inventory of finished goods		xxxx	xxxx
Gross profit			xxxx

The profit and loss account section will include only office, selling and financial expenses.

The balance sheet of a manufacturing business follows the same format as that of any other form of business. The only difference is that there may be three inventories rather than one.

Example 2.6

Financial statements of a non-trading organisation:
The treasurer of a non-trading organisation usually prepares a summary of the cash book which is known as a receipts and payments account. This shows all money received on the debit side and all money paid out on the credit side and is balanced in the same way as a cash account.

A trading account section of an income statement may be prepared if the organisation operates a shop or café etc where goods are bought and sold. This is very similar to the trading account section of an income statement of a business.

Non-trading Organisation
Shop Income Statement for the year ended ....

	$	$	$
Revenue (Sales)			XXXX
Less Cost of sales			
Opening inventory		XXXX	
Purchases		XXXX	
		XXXX	
Less Closing inventory		XXXX	
Cost of goods sold		XXXX	
Add Shop expenses			
Wages of shop assistant	XXXX		
Shop rent and rates	XXXX		
Depreciation of shop fittings	XXXX	XXXX	XXXX
Profit on shop			XXXX

The treasurer will prepare the equivalent of the profit and loss account section of an income statement of a business which is known as an income and expenditure account. This follows the same format as a profit and loss account section of an income statement. The expenses of the organisation are deducted from the revenue. The resulting figure is referred to as a surplus or deficit rather than a profit or loss.

Non-trading Organisation
Income and Expenditure Account for the year ended ....

	$	$	$
Income			
Subscriptions			XXXX
Profit on shop			XXXX
Competition – entrance fees		XXXX	
less expenses		XXXX	XXXX
Interest received			XXXX
*Profit on disposal of non-current assets			XXXX
			XXXX
Expenditure			
General expenses		XXXX	
Rates and insurance		XXXX	
Repairs and maintenance		XXXX	
Loan interest		XXXX	
*Loss on disposal of non-current assets		XXXX	
Depreciation of equipment		XXXX	XXXX
**Surplus for the year			XXXX

  * If only one asset was sold during the year only one of these items will appear.
  ** If the expenditure exceeds the income, the resulting figure is described as a deficit.

14 *Cambridge O Level Principles of Accounts Workbook*

The first section of the balance sheet of a non-trading organisation follows the same format as that of a sole trader. The second section of the balance sheet has to be modified so that it shows the accumulated fund and the surplus or deficit.

Non-trading Organisation
Extract from Balance Sheet at ....

	$	$	$
Accumulated fund			
Opening balance			xxxx
*Plus surplus for the year			xxxx
			xxxx

*If there is a deficit this will be deducted rather than added.

Section 3

Examples of Questions and Answers

Before starting to answer an accounting question, think carefully and read both the data and the requirements. No marks will be gained for an answer which does not answer the question being asked!

If separate stationery is provided in an examination, it is often useful to use a separate sheet for workings – where answers have to be written on the actual question paper there are often blank pages which can be used for workings. It is often necessary to switch between the actual answer sheet and the workings during the course of answering the question. If workings are clearly labelled, marks may be awarded even if the final "answer" is incorrect.

Below are three examples of typical examination questions. They are accompanied by suggested answers and an outline of the stages involved in preparing those answers.

Example 3.1

Chao is a business advisor. He provided the following trial balance at 31 July 20-8.

	$		$
Salaries	52 000	Fees from clients	120 000
Rates and insurance	7 100	Provision for doubtful debts	880
Advertising	9 400	Provision for depreciation	
Motor expenses	3 100	of equipment	980
General office expenses	17 236	Provision for depreciation	
Premises at cost	60 000	of motor vehicles	5 250
Equipment at cost	9 800	Loan (5% pa) repayable	
Motor vehicles at cost	12 000	31 December 20-9	20 000
Trade receivables	31 000	Capital	79 000
Drawings	42 000	Bank overdraft	17 526
	243 636		243 636

16   *Cambridge O Level Principles of Accounts Workbook*

The following additional information is also provided.

1   At 31 July 20-8–
    salaries accrued amounted to $2100
    rates prepaid amounted to $210
    one year's interest is accrued on the loan
2   The equipment is to be depreciated at 10% per annum using the straight line method.
    The motor vehicles are to be depreciated at 20% per annum using the reducing balance method.
3   Bad debts of $300 are to be written off.
    The provision for doubtful debts is to be adjusted to 2% of the remaining Trade receivables.

(a) Prepare the income statement of Chao for the year ended 31 July 20-8.
(b) Prepare the balance sheet of Chao at 31 July 20-8.

Answer

(a)

Chao
Income Statement for the year ended 31 July 20-8

	$	$
Fees from clients		120 000
Add Reduction in provision for doubtful debts (880 – 614)		266
		120 266
Less Salaries (52 000 + 2100)	54 100	
Rates and insurance (7100 – 210)	6 890	
Advertising	9 400	
Motor expenses	3 100	
General office expenses	17 236	
Bad debts	300	
Loan interest	1 000	
Depreciation of equipment (10% × 9800)	980	
Depreciation of motor vehicles (20% × (12 000 – 5250))	1 350	94 356
Profit for the year		25 910

(b)

Chao
Balance Sheet at 31 July 20-8

Non-current assets	$ Cost	$ Depreciation to date	$ Book value
Premises	60 000		60 000
Equipment	9 800	1 960	7 840
Motor vehicles	12 000	6 600	5 400
	81 800	8 560	73 240
Current assets			
Trade receivables	30 700		
Less Provision for doubtful debts	614	30 086	
Other receivables		210	
		30 296	

(Continued)

Current liabilities			
Other payables	3 100		
Bank overdraft	17 526	20 626	
Net current assets			9 670
			82 910
Non-current liabilities			
Loan (repayable 31 December 20-9)			20 000
			62 910
Financed by			
Capital			
Opening balance			79 000
Profit for the year			25 910
			104 910
Less Drawings			42 000
			62 910

The stages in producing the answer

1. Go through the trial balance and the accompanying notes and label all the items.

Put a label "IS" against anything which will be used in the income statement.

Put a label "BS" against anything which will be used in the balance sheet.

Remember that anything in the trial balance is used once in a set of financial statements and any notes to a trial balance are used twice.

The items should be labelled as follows.

		$			$
IS	Salaries	52 000	**IS**	Fees from clients	120 000
IS	Rates and insurance	7 100	**IS**	Provision for doubtful debts	880
IS	Advertising	9 400	**BS**	Provision for depreciation	
IS	Motor expenses	3 100		of equipment	980
IS	General office expenses	17 236	**BS**	Provision for depreciation	
BS	Premises at cost	60 000		of motor vehicles	5 250
BS	Equipment at cost	9 800	**BS**	Loan (5% pa) repayable	
BS	Motor vehicles at cost	12 000		31 December 20-9	20 000
BS	Trade receivables	31 000	**BS**	Capital	79 000
BS	Drawings	42 000	**BS**	Bank overdraft	17 526
		243 636			243 636

	1	At 31 July 20-8	
IS BS		salaries accrued amounted to $2100	
IS BS		rates prepaid amounted to $210	
IS BS		one year's interest is accrued on the loan	
IS BS	2	The equipment is to be depreciated at 10% per annum using the straight line method.	
IS BS		The motor vehicles are to be depreciated at 20% per annum using the reducing balance method.	
IS BS	3	Bad debts of $300 are to be written off.	
IS BS		The provision for doubtful debts is to be adjusted to 2% of the remaining trade receivables.	

18   *Cambridge O Level Principles of Accounts Workbook*

2. Prepare the income statement.

Tick off the items as they are used to ensure that nothing is omitted.

The trial balance and accompanying notes should now appear as follows.

		$				$
✔ **IS**	Salaries	52 000	✔ **IS**	Fees from clients		120 000
✔ **IS**	Rates and insurance	7 100	✔ **IS**	Provision for doubtful debts		880
✔ **IS**	Advertising	9 400	**BS**	Provision for depreciation		
✔ **IS**	Motor expenses	3 100		of equipment		980
✔ **IS**	General office expenses	17 236	**BS**	Provision for depreciation		
BS	Premises at cost	60 000		of motor vehicles		5 250
BS	Equipment at cost	9 800	**BS**	Loan (5% pa) repayable		
BS	Motor vehicles at cost	12 000		31 December 20-9		20 000
BS	Trade receivables	31 000	**BS**	Capital		79 000
BS	Drawings	42 000	**BS**	Bank overdraft		17 526
		243 636				243 636

	1	At 31 July 20-8
✔ **IS BS**		salaries accrued amounted to $2100
✔ **IS BS**		rates prepaid amounted to $210
✔ **IS BS**		one year's interest is accrued on the loan
✔ **IS BS**	2	The equipment is to be depreciated at 10% per annum using the straight line method.
✔ **IS BS**		The motor vehicles are to be depreciated at 20% per annum using the reducing balance method.
✔ **IS BS**	3	Bad debts of $300 are to be written off.
✔ **IS BS**		The provision for doubtful debts is to be adjusted to 2% of the remaining trade receivables.

Remember that the exiting provision for doubtful debts only appears in the income statement as part of the calculation of the amount which is surplus to requirements.

3. Prepare the balance sheet.

Tick off the items as they are used to ensure that nothing is omitted.

The trial balance and accompanying notes should now appear as follows.

		$				$
✔ **IS**	Salaries	52 000	✔ **IS**	Fees from clients		120 000
✔ **IS**	Rates and insurance	7 100	✔ **IS**	Provision for doubtful debts		880
✔ **IS**	Advertising	9 400	✔ **BS**	Provision for depreciation		
✔ **IS**	Motor expenses	3 100		of equipment		980
✔ **IS**	General office expenses	17 236	✔ **BS**	Provision for depreciation		
✔ **BS**	Premises at cost	60 000		of motor vehicles		5 250
✔ **BS**	Equipment at cost	9 800	✔ **BS**	Loan (5% pa) repayable		
✔ **BS**	Motor vehicles at cost	12 000		31 December 20-9		20 000
✔ **BS**	Trade receivables	31 000	✔ **BS**	Capital		79 000
✔ **BS**	Drawings	42 000	✔ **BS**	Bank overdraft		17 526
		243 636				243 636

			1	At 31 July 20-8
✔ ✔	**IS BS**			salaries accrued amounted to $2100
✔ ✔	**IS BS**			rates prepaid amounted to $210
✔ ✔	**IS BS**			one year's interest is accrued on the loan
✔ ✔	**IS BS**	2		The equipment is to be depreciated at 10% per annum using the straight line method.
✔ ✔	**IS BS**			The motor vehicles are to be depreciated at 20% per annum using the reducing balance method.
✔ ✔	**IS BS**	3		Bad debts of $300 are to be written off.
✔ ✔	**IS BS**			The provision for doubtful debts is to be adjusted to 2% of the remaining trade receivables.

Example 3.2

At the end of her financial year on 31 May 20-9, the totals of Rita's trial balance failed to balance. The total of the debit side was $98 730 and the total of the credit side was $99 176. She entered the difference in a suspense account and prepared a draft income statement. The profit for the year was calculated at $9366.

The following errors were then discovered.

1. An invoice for goods sold on credit to Waqas had been entered in the sales journal as $1100 instead of $110.

2. The purchases returns journal had been overcast by $100.

3. A new motor vehicle was purchased on 30 May 20-9. The total cost, $12 650, which included $340 for fuel and insurance, had been debited to the motor vehicles account. No depreciation is required for the motor vehicle for the year ended 31 May 20-9.

4. The total of the discount received column in the cash book, $82, had been debited to the discount allowed account in the ledger.

5. The balance of the cash column of the cash book, $50, had been omitted from the trial balance.

6. Bower Ltd. is both a supplier and a customer. Sales, $230, on credit to Bower Ltd. had been credited to the account of Bower Ltd. in the purchases ledger.

(a) Prepare journal entries to correct errors 1–6 above. Narratives are not required.

(b) Write up the suspense account showing all the necessary corrections. Start with the balance arising from the difference on the trial balance.

(c) Prepare a statement to show the corrected profit for the year ended 31 May 20-9.

20 Cambridge O Level Principles of Accounts Workbook

Answer

(a)

Rita
Journal

		Debit $	Credit $
1	Sales	990	
	Waqas		990
2	Purchases returns	100	
	Suspense		100
3	Motor vehicle expenses	340	
	Motor vehicle		340
4	Suspense	164	
	Discount allowed		82
	Discount received		82
5	–		
	Suspense		50
6	Bower Ltd (purchases ledger)	230	
	Bower Ltd (sales ledger)	230	
	Suspense		460

(b)

Rita
Suspense account

Date	Details	Folio	$	Date	Details	Folio	$
20-9				20-9			
May 31	Difference on			May 31	Purchases returns		100
	trial balance		446		Petty cash		50
	Discount allowed		82		Bower Ltd.		
	Discount received		82		(Purchases		
					Ledger)		230
					Bower Ltd.		
					(Sales Ledger)		230
			610				610

(c)

Rita
Statement of corrected profit for the year ended 31 May 20-9

	$	$
Profit for the year		9366
Add Discount received understated	82	
Discount allowed overstated	82	164
		9530
Less Sales overstated	990	
Purchases returns overcast	100	
Motor vehicle expenses understated	340	1430
Corrected profit for the year		8100

The stages in producing the answer

(a) Journal entries

1. An invoice for goods sold on credit to Waqas had been entered in the sales journal as $1100 instead of $110.

The entries made –
There was an error in the sales journal. The incorrect figure would have been posted to the account of Waqas and the total sales transferred to the sales account would also be incorrect. Ignoring any other items, the entries made were –

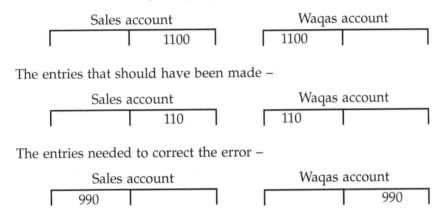

Sales account		Waqas account	
	1100	1100	

The entries that should have been made –

Sales account		Waqas account	
	110	110	

The entries needed to correct the error –

Sales account		Waqas account	
990			990

A journal entry can now be made debiting the sales account and crediting Waqas account with $990. This will result in a net entry of $110 on the correct side of each account.

The trial balance totals are not affected so an entry in the suspense account is not needed.

2. The purchases returns journal had been overcast by $100.

The entry made –
The incorrect figure for the total of the purchases returns journal would have been credited to the purchases returns account. Ignoring any other items, the entry made was –

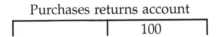

Purchases returns account	
	100

There are no errors on the debit side as only the total of the purchases journal is incorrect.

The entries needed to correct the error –

Purchases returns account		Suspense account	
100			100

Because this error was only on one side of the ledger, it affected the balancing of the trial balance. An entry in the suspense account must be made to make a double entry for debit of $100.

A journal entry can now be made debiting the purchases returns account and crediting the suspense account with $100.

3. **A new motor vehicle was purchased on 30 May 20-9. The total cost, $12 650, which included $340 for fuel and insurance, had been debited to the motor vehicles account.**

   No depreciation is required for the motor vehicle for the year ended 31 May 20-9.

   The entry made –

Motor vehicle account	
12 650	

   The total cost was debited to the motor vehicle expenses account.
   The entries that should have been made –

Motor vehicle account			Motor vehicle expenses account	
12 310			340	

   The entries needed to correct the error –

Motor vehicle account			Motor vehicle expenses account	
	340			340

   A journal entry can now be made debiting the motor vehicle account and crediting the motor vehicle expenses account with $340.

   The trial balance totals are not affected so an entry in the suspense account is not needed.

4. **The total of the discount received column in the cash book, $82, had been debited to the discount allowed account in the ledger.**

   The entry made –
   Ignoring any other items, the entry was –

Discount allowed account	
82	

   The entry that should have been made –

Discount received account	
	82

   There were no errors in the individual purchases ledger accounts as only the total of the column was treated incorrectly.

   The entries needed to correct the error –

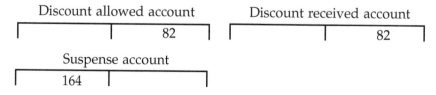

Because this error resulted in an amount being debited that should have been credited, it affected the balancing of the trial balance. An entry in the suspense account must be made of $164 to make a double entry for the two credits of $82.

A journal entry can now be made debiting the suspense account with $164 and crediting both the discount allowed account and the discount received account with $82.

5. **The balance of the cash column of the cash book, $50, had been omitted from the trial balance.**

No errors of double entry were made. The only error made was to omit a balance from the trial balance.

The entries needed to correct this error –
Insert the cash balance in the debit column of the trial balance.

This error affected the balancing of the trial balance. An entry in the suspense account must be made.

```
        Suspense account
                |   50
```

A single-sided journal entry can now be made crediting the suspense account with $50.

6. **Bower Ltd is both a supplier and a customer. Sales, $230, on credit to Bower Ltd had been credited to the account of Bower Ltd in the purchases ledger.**

The entry made –
Ignoring any other items, the entry was –

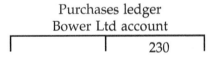

The entry that should have been made –

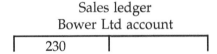

The entries needed to correct the error –

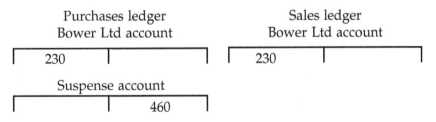

Because this error resulted in an amount being credited that should have been debited, it affected the balancing of the trial balance. An entry in the suspense account must be made of $460 to make a double entry for the two debits of $230.

24 *Cambridge O Level Principles of Accounts Workbook*

A journal entry can now be made by debiting both Bower Ltd's account in the purchases ledger and Bower Ltd's account in the sales ledger with $230 and crediting the suspense account with $460.

(b) Suspense account

Calculate the difference between the totals of the trial balance. Enter this figure on the debit side of the suspense account.
Refer back to the calculations and the journal entries and make the appropriate entries in the suspense account. Total the account.

(c) Statement of corrected profit for the year

Consider each error –

1. **An invoice for goods sold on credit to Waqas had been entered in the sales journal as $1100 instead of $110.**
   Correcting this error reduces the sales. This means that the profit will also reduce. This item should be deducted from the profit for the year.

2. **The purchases returns journal had been overcast by $100.**
   Correcting this error reduces the purchases returns, which, in turn increases the net purchases. This means that the profit will reduce.
   This item should be deducted from the profit for the year.

3. **A new motor vehicle was purchased on 30 May 20-9. The total cost, $12 650, which included $340 for fuel and insurance, had been debited to the motor vehicles account.**
   No depreciation is required for the motor vehicle for the year ended 31 May 20-9.
   Correcting this error increases the motor vehicle expenses. This means that the profit will reduce.
   This item should be deducted from the profit for the year.
   (If the motor vehicle had been purchased earlier in the year and depreciation was required, this would have to be adjusted as the calculation would have been made on $12 650 rather than the correct figure of $12 310.)

4. **The total of the discount received column in the cash book, $82, had been debited to the discount allowed account in the ledger.**
   Correcting this error increases the discount received. This means that the profit will also increase. The correction also reduces the discount allowed. This means that the profit will increase.
   This means that both of these items should be added to the profit for the year.

5. **The balance of the cash column of the cash book, $50, had been omitted from the trial balance.**
   Correcting this error does not affect any items in the income statement so the profit is not affected.

Examples of Questions and Answers   25

6. **Bower Ltd is both a supplier and a customer. Sales, $230, on credit to Bower Ltd had been credited to the account of Bower Ltd in the purchases ledger.**

Correcting this error does not affect any items in the income statement so the profit is not affected.

Write down the profit for the year shown in the draft statement.
Add the items which increase the profit for the year.
Deduct the items which reduce the profit for the year.
Calculate the corrected profit for the year.

Example 3.3

Ashok started business on 1 January 20-2 with a capital of $26 000. This consisted of equipment, $9000, a motor vehicle, $12 000, and the remainder in cash which was paid into a business bank account.

Ashok did not maintain any accounting records, but was able to provide the following information at the end of his first month of trading on 31 January 20-2.

		$
1	Cheques received and paid into the bank	
	Credit customers	4000
2	Payments by cheque	
	Credit suppliers	4200
	Wages	800
	Rent and rates	300
	Insurance	95
	Office cash	400
3	Cash receipts	
	Bank	400
	Cash sales	2400
4	Cash payments	
	Cash purchases	500
	General expenses	890
5	Ashok failed to calculate the value of his inventory on 31 January 20-2. All goods were sold at a mark up of 50%.	
6	During the month of January 20-2	
	Ashok took goods, at cost, for his own use	300
	Sales returns amounted to	240
	Purchases returns amounted to	950
	Bad debts written off amounted to	160
7	At 31 January 20-2	
	Trade receivables amounted to	2110
	Trade payables amounted to	2650
8	Ashok decided to depreciate his non-current assets as follows:	
	Equipment at 10% per annum on cost	
	Motor vehicle at 20% per annum on cost	

26 *Cambridge O Level Principles of Accounts Workbook*

(a) Prepare the income statement of Ashok for the month ended 31 January 20-2.

(b) Prepare the balance sheet of Ashok at 31 January 20-2.

Answer

(a)

Ashok

Income Statement for the month ended 31 January 20-2

	$	$	$
Revenue (Sales)		8910	
Less Sales returns		240	8670
Less Cost of sales			
Purchases	8300		
Less Purchases returns	950		
	7350		
Less goods for own use	300	7050	
Closing inventory		1270	5780
Gross profit			2890
Less Wages		800	
Rent and rates		300	
Insurance		95	
General expenses		890	
Bad debts		160	
Depreciation of equipment		75	
Deprecation of motor vehicle		200	2520
Profit for the month			370

(b)

Ashok

Balance Sheet at 31 January 20-2

Non-current assets	$ Cost	$ Depreciation to date	$ Book value
Equipment	9 000	75	8 925
Motor vehicle	12 000	200	11 800
	21 000	275	20 725
Current assets			
Inventory		1 270	
Trade receivables		2 110	
Bank		3 205	
Cash		1 410	
		7 995	
Current liabilities			
Trade payables		2 650	
Net current assets			5 345
			26 070
Financed by			
Capital			
Opening balance			26 000
Plus Profit for the month			370
			26 370
Less Drawings			300
			26 070

Examples of Questions and Answers   27

The stages in producing the answer

(a) Income statement

1 Calculate the revenue (sales).

Total trade receivables account

Date	Details	Folio	$	Date	Details	Folio	$
20-2				20-2			
Jan 31	Sales*		6510	Jan 31	Bank		4000
					Returns		240
					Bad debts		160
					Balance	c/d	2110
			6510				6510
20-2							
Feb 1	Balance	b/d	2110				

	$
Total revenue (sales)	
Credit sales	6510
Cash sales	2400
	8910

2 Calculate the purchases.

Total trade payables account

Date	Details	Folio	$	Date	Details	Folio	$
20-2				20-2			
Jan 31	Bank		4200	Jan 31	Purchases *		7800
	Returns		950				
	Balance	c/d	2650				
			7800				7800
				20-2			
				Feb 1	Balance	b/d	2650

	$
Total purchases	
Credit purchases	7800
Cash purchases	500
	8300

3 Enter the sales and purchases in the income statement.
Remember to also enter the sales returns, purchases returns and goods taken for own use.
Calculate and enter the gross profit. The mark up is 50% so the gross profit will be 50/150 × the sales i.e. 1/3 of the sales.
Working "backwards" the missing figure of closing inventory can be inserted.

28   *Cambridge O Level Principles of Accounts Workbook*

4   Calculate the depreciation. Remember that statements are for one month only.
Equipment   10% × \$9000 × 1/12   = \$90
Motor vehicle   20% × \$12 000 × 1/12 = \$200

5   Enter the expenses in the income statement.
Remember to include the general expenses paid in cash and the bad debts. Calculate the profit for the month.

(b) Balance sheet

1 Calculate the bank balance.

Bank account

Date	Details	Folio	$	Date	Details	Folio	$
20-2				20-2			
Jan 1	Capital		5000	Jan 31	Total payments		5795
31	Total receipts		4000		Balance	c/d	3205
			9000				9000
20-2							
Feb 1	Balance	b/d	3205				

2 Calculate the cash balance.

Cash account

Date	Details	Folio	$	Date	Details	Folio	$
20-2				20-2			
Jan 31	Total receipts		2800	Jan 31	Total payments		1390
					Balance	c/d	1410
			2800				2800
20-2							
Feb 1	Balance	b/d	1410				

3 Prepare the balance sheet.

Section 4

Short Questions on Accounting Terminology

Before sitting for an accounting examination, a thorough knowledge of the words and terms used in accounting is necessary. This section concentrates on short questions involving words and phrases which are frequently used in accounting.

The answers to the following questions can be found by looking up the appropriate word or phrase in the textbook *Cambridge O Level Principles of Accounts*.

Part 1

Explain the difference between each of the following pairs of words or phrases.
- **(a)** Assets and liabilities
- **(b)** Carriage inwards and carriage outwards
- **(c)** Debit note and credit note
- **(d)** Gross profit and net profit
- **(e)** Service business and trading business
- **(f)** Capital expenditure and revenue expenditure
- **(g)** Bad debts and provision for doubtful debts
- **(h)** Bank statement and bank reconciliation statement
- **(i)** Margin and mark-up
- **(j)** Turnover and rate of turnover
- **(k)** Partner's capital account and partner's current account
- **(l)** Prime cost and cost of production
- **(m)** Called up share capital and paid up share capital
- **(n)** Preference shares and ordinary shares
- **(o)** Capital owned and capital employed
- **(p)** Current ratio and quick ratio

30 *Cambridge O Level Principles of Accounts Workbook*

(q) Time basis and piece basis of calculating pay
(r) Statutory and voluntary deductions from wages
(s) Gross pay and net pay
(t) Payroll and payslip

Part 2

Provide a definition of each of the following words or phrases.

(a) Capital
(b) Balance sheet
(c) Three column running balance ledger account
(d) Bank overdraft
(e) Contra entry
(f) Trial balance
(g) Net current assets
(h) Prudence
(i) Going concern
(j) Accrued expense
(k) Prepaid income
(l) Depreciation
(m) Narrative in connection with a journal entry
(n) Control account
(o) Accumulated fund
(p) Goodwill
(q) Direct expense of manufacturing
(r) Departmental income statement
(s) Professional ethics

Part 3

Insert the appropriate word or words to complete the following sentences.

(a) ....is concerned with the detailed recording of the financial transactions of a business .... uses these detailed records to prepare financial statements at regular intervals.

(b) The two effects of every financial transaction are recorded using a method of .... bookkeeping.

(c) A list of the balances on the accounts in the ledger on a certain date is known as a ....

(d) An entry made on the correct side and using the correct amount, but in the wrong class of account is known as an error of ....

(e) When the correct amount is entered in the correct accounts, but on the wrong side of each account this is known as an error of ....

(f) The accounts of .... are kept in the sales ledger and the accounts of ....are kept in the purchases ledger.

(g) A cheque which a debtor's bank refuses to pay because of lack of funds is known as a ....cheque.

(h) Cash withdrawn from bank for office use is .... in the .... column and .... in the .... column.

(i) A .... is an acknowledgement of money received.

(j) The total of the sales journal is transferred to the .... side of the ....account at the end of each month.

(k) The name of the book of prime entry in which returns to credit suppliers are recorded is the .... journal.

(l) The principle which states that the business is treated as being completely separate from the owner of the business is known as the .... principle.

(m) Inventory should be valued at the lower of .... and ....

(n) The method of depreciation when the annual charge is calculated on the cost of the asset less depreciation previously written off is known as the .... method of depreciation.

(o) A cheque which the payee has not yet paid into his bank is known as a cheque not yet ....

(p) A summary of the cash book of a non-trading organisation is known as a......................... and .... account.

(q) Amounts paid by the members of a society, usually annually, to use the facilities provided by the society are known as ....

(r) Partners may be entitled to .... on .... as a reward for investing in the business rather than elsewhere.

(s) .... are long term loans in a limited company.

Section 5

Structured Accounting Questions

This section consists of examination-style questions to complement those in the textbook *O Level Principles of Accounts*. The topics are arranged in the same order as those in the textbook. For reference purposes, the chapter headings of the textbook are provided. The summarised answers for most of the questions are given in Appendix 1. Answers for the questions marked with an asterisk (*) are available in a teachers' supplement.

Chapter 1   Introduction to Accounting

1. Explain the difference between bookkeeping and accounting.
2. (a) State the formula for the accounting equation.
   (b) Fill in the blanks in the following table.

	Capital $	Assets $	Liabilities $
(i)	....	50 000	15 000
(ii)	140 000	....	52 000
(iii)	45 000	68 000	....
(iv)	....	99 000	27 000

Structured Accounting Questions 33

3. Indicate whether **each** of the following is an asset or a liability of Anna who owns a general store. The first one has been done for you as an example.

Item	Asset	Liability
(a) Fittings	✓	
(b) Cash		
(c) Inventory of goods		
(d) Trade payables		
(e) Trade receivables		
(f) Motor vehicle		
(g) Loan to employee		

4. State how **each** of the following transactions affect the assets and liabilities of Mahesh who owns a factory. The first one has been done for you as an example.

	Transaction	Effect on assets	Effect on liabilities
(a)	Bought goods for cash	Cash Decrease Inventory Increase	No effect
(b)	Bought machine on credit	....	....
(c)	Paid creditor by cheque	....	....
(d)	Made a cash loan to employee	....	....
(e)	Received a long term bank loan	....	....

5. The balance sheet of Mary on 1 January 20-9 is shown below.

Mary
Balance Sheet at 1 January 20-9

Assets	$	Liabilities	$
Premises	100 000	Capital	158 000
Fixtures	30 000	Trade payables	12 000
Inventory	18 000		
Trade receivables	13 000		
Bank	9 000		
	170 000		170 000

34 *Cambridge O Level Principles of Accounts Workbook*

On 2 January 20-9 the following transactions took place.
(a) Bought goods, $1500, on credit
(b) A credit customer paid $500 by cheque
(c) Mary invested a further $10 000 by cheque
(d) Additional fixtures, $1000, were bought on credit
Prepare the balance sheet of Mary on 2 January 20-9 after the above transactions have taken place.

*6. Kumar is a trader. On 1 August 20-8 his balance sheet was as follows.

Kumar
Balance Sheet at 1 August 20-8

Assets	$	Liabilities	$
Machinery	55 000	Capital	80 000
Equipment	18 000	Loan	20 000
Motor vehicle	15 000	Trade payables	9 200
Inventory	9 500		
Trade receivables	6 500		
Bank	5 200		
	109 200		109 200

On 2 August 20-8 the following transactions took place.
(a) Paid a credit supplier $2100 by cheque
(b) A credit customer paid $100 in cash
(c) Purchased goods, $1500, and paid by cheque
(d) Borrowed a further $10 000 and purchased an additional motor vehicle

Prepare the balance sheet of Kumar on 2 August 20-8 after the above transactions have taken place.

Chapter 2   Double Entry Bookkeeping – Part A

7. For **each** of the following transactions insert the name of the account to be debited and the name of the account to be credited.

	Transaction	Account to be debited	Account to be credited
(a)	Paid rent by cheque	....	....
(b)	Bought goods for cash	....	....
(c)	Paid cash for carriage on goods bought	....	....
(d)	Bought equipment on credit from WR Stores	....	....
(e)	Sold goods on credit to Jones	....	....
(f)	Jones returned goods	....	....
(g)	The owner took goods for his own use	....	....

Structured Accounting Questions 35

8. Raminder provided the following information for March 20-9.

			$
March	1	Balance of cash	100
		Balance at bank	2750
	4	Received cheque from Wahid, a debtor	280
	9	Paid office expenses in cash	22
	13	Received a loan from AB Loans by cheque	5000
	18	Purchased equipment and paid by cheque	4500
	24	Received commission by cheque	150
	28	Paid Sabena, a creditor, by cheque	330
	31	Cash sales	840
		Raminder took cash for personal use	200

Record the above transactions in Raminder's cash account and bank account. Balance the accounts on 31 March and bring down the balances on 1 April 20-9.

9. Mona started a business on 1 January 20-4. The following are her transactions for the first two weeks of trading.

January	1	Capital, $20 000, was paid into a business bank account
		Paid rent, $500, by cheque
	2	Bought goods, $3300, on credit from Mohamed
	4	Returned goods, $100, to Mohamed
	7	Sold goods, $1700, on credit to Aswan Traders
	9	Received $120 commission in cash
	10	Paid Mohamed $3000 by cheque on account
	12	Aswan Traders paid $1000 by cheque on account
	13	Paid sundry expenses in cash $20
	14	Cash sales, $1500
		Cash withdrawn for personal use, $500

Enter the above transactions in the ledger of Mona. Balance the cash account, the bank account, and the accounts of Mohamed and Aswan Traders on 14 January and bring down the balances on 15 January 20-4.

10. **(a)** From the following information, write up the account of Sanele in the books of Thomas for the month of July 20-1. Prepare the account in three column running balance format.

June	1	Sanele owed Thomas $450
	6	Sanele purchased goods, $1200, on credit from Thomas
	10	Sanele returned goods, $50, to Thomas
	14	Sanele paid $250 to Thomas in cash
	20	Sanele purchased goods, $590, on credit from Thomas
	26	Sanele paid $1000 by cheque to Thomas

(b) State **one** advantage of using the three column running balance format for ledger accounts.

36 *Cambridge O Level Principles of Accounts Workbook*

*11. Jason started a business on 1 April 20-5. His transactions for the first month of trading were as follows:

April 1 Jason introduced capital of $40 000. Of this $1000 was in cash. The remainder was paid into the business bank account
2 Purchased premises, $25 000, by cheque
4 Purchased goods, $9500, on credit from Lynne
6 Paid general expenses, $250, in cash
9 Cash sales, $320
12 Sold goods, $1460, on credit to Paul
Paid $10, in cash, for carriage on sales
15 Paul returned goods, $120
20 Jason took goods, $100, for his own use
24 Paid Lynne $8000, on account, by cheque
27 Paul paid the amount outstanding by cheque
28 Received a long term loan, $10 000, by cheque, from ABC Finance
30 Paid assistant's wages in cash, $200

Enter the above transactions in the ledger of Jason. Balance the cash account, the bank account, and the accounts of Lynne and Paul on 30 April and bring down the balances on 1 May 20-5.

12. The following accounts appear in the ledger of Akinola. Explain **each** entry in **each** of the accounts and also state where the double entry for **each** entry will be found.

(a)

Akinola
Anwar account

Date	Details	Folio	$	Date	Details	Folio	$
20-6				20-6			
Mar 1	Balance	b/d	250	Mar 12	Returns		30
9	Sales		870	18	Bank		800
				31	Balance	c/d	290
			1120				1120
20-6							
Apl 1	Balance	b/d	290				

(b)

Akinola
Drawings account

Date	Details	Folio	$	Date	Details	Folio	$
20-6				20-6			
Mar 10	Bank		100	Mar 31	Capital		365
28	Purchases		265				
			365				365

Chapter 3 The Trial Balance

13. (a) State **two** uses of a trial balance.
(b) Name and explain **two** errors which a trial balance will not reveal.

Structured Accounting Questions 37

(c) Explain which of the following errors would be revealed by a trial balance. Give a reason for your answer.

Error 1 Goods sold on credit to Appiah, $950, were recorded in the sales journal as $590.

Error 2 Goods sold on credit to Appiah, $600, were omitted from Appiah's account.

Error 3 Goods sold on credit to Appiah, $720, were omitted from the books.

14. The following balances were extracted from the books of Peter Mutanda on 31 October 20-2.

	$
Cash	600
Bank overdraft	10 500
Equipment	18 200
Fixtures and fittings	6 100
Trade receivables	12 400
Trade payables	13 600
Purchases	48 600
Sales	66 200
Sales returns	3 300
Wages	21 400
Office expenses	4 700
Carriage inwards	900
Sundry expenses	4 000
Drawings	12 500
Capital	?

Prepare Peter Mutanda's trial balance at 31 October 20-2 showing his capital account balance.

15. An inexperienced bookkeeper prepared the following trial balance of Maria Motoso. The bookkeeper placed various balances in the wrong column.

	$	$
Premises		60 000
Fixtures and fittings	13 500	
Inventory 1 January 20-4		9 500
Trade receivables		14 200
Trade payables	9 800	
Cash at bank		2 300
Loan from XY Finance	5 000	
Purchases		36 100
Sales	45 900	
Sales returns		1 400
Rent and rates	4 700	
Wages	12 300	
General expenses	2 500	
Carriage outwards		2 600
Capital – balancing figure	32 400	
	126 100	126 100

Prepare Maria Motoso's amended trial balance at 31 December 20-4, showing the correct capital account balance.

38 Cambridge O Level Principles of Accounts Workbook

*16. John Ameobi is a trader. He has little knowledge of accounting, but attempted to prepare a trial balance at the end of his financial year. The trial balance he prepared is shown below.

John Ameobi
Trial Balance for the year ended 30 November 20-8

	Debit $	Credit $
Purchases		174 900
Sales	246 500	
Carriage inwards	5 650	
Carriage outwards		4 210
Bank overdraft	14 500	
Sundry expenses		3 600
Equipment	5 700	
Motor vehicles	10 400	
Salaries		62 590
Trade receivables		21 610
Trade payables	16 440	
Rent and rates	7 990	
Insurance		3 200
Inventory 1 December 20-7	14 850	
Loan to employee		1 000
Capital (balancing figure)		50 920
	322 030	322 030

In addition to the obvious errors in the above trial balance, the following errors have also been discovered:

1 Drawings, $4100, have been omitted from the trial balance
2 A cheque, $90, paid to Chan, a creditor, has been debited to Chen's account
3 Both the salaries account and the purchases account have been undercast by $1000
4 No entry has been made for sundry expenses, $2150, paid by cheque

(a) State how **each** of the above errors will affect the trial balance. Give a reason for your answer in each case.
(b) Prepare an amended trial balance for John Ameobi at 30 November 20-8.

Chapter 4 Double Entry Bookkeeping – Part B

17. (a) State **one** reason why the ledger is often divided into specialised areas.
(b) Complete the following table and indicate in which ledger of a trader the following accounts would be recorded. The first has been done for you as an example.

	Account	Sales ledger	Purchases ledger	Nominal ledger
(i)	Wages			✓
(ii)	Sales			
(iii)	Inventory			
(iv)	Hassan, a debtor			
(v)	Khan, a creditor			
(vi)	Drawings			

Structured Accounting Questions 39

18. The balances on Anjori's cash and bank accounts on 1 May 20-9 were:

		$
Cash		200
Bank		4960

The following transactions took place during the month.

May 4 Paid Western Stores $2120 by cheque
     9 Received a cheque, $1310, from C Wright
    13 Cash sales, $950
    15 Paid $40 in cash for carriage on sales
    19 Paid $900 cash into bank
    22 Anjori withdrew $500 from the bank for her own use
    26 Paid insurance, $1420, by cheque
    30 Purchased a motor vehicle, $5500, and paid by cheque

(a) Record the transactions for May in Anjori's cash book and bring down the balances on 1 June 20-9.
(b) Explain the meaning of the word "contra" when used in connection with cash books.
(c) Explain why it is **not** possible to have a credit balance brought down on a cash account.
(d) State whether the cash balance and the bank balance in Anjori's cash book at the end of May 20-9 represent assets or liabilities.

19. Vikram's financial year ends on 30 November. The balances in his cash book on 1 November 20-3 were as follows:

		$
Cash		135
Bank overdraft		3150

The following transactions took place in November 20-3.

November   7 Received a cheque, $50, from High Street Stores
          14 The bank returned High Street Stores' cheque as dishonoured
          17 Cash sales, $1670, paid directly into the bank
          20 Paid Marine Traders $936 by cheque after deducting $24 cash discount
          23 Paid a cheque to Seafresh Foods in settlement of their account of $750 less 2% discount
          26 Received a cheque from Valley Stores in settlement of their debt of $200 less 4% cash discount
          29 Withdrew $1000 cash from bank for business use
          30 Paid wages, $860, in cash

(a) Record the transactions for November 20-3 in Vikram's three column cash book. Balance the cash and bank columns and bring down the balances on 1 December 20-3.
(b) Explain why a trader may grant cash discount.

40 *Cambridge O Level Principles of Accounts Workbook*

(c) Calculate the percentage of cash discount Vikram deducted when he paid Marine Traders on 20 November.

(d) Explain the entry that should be made in the ledger on 26 November in respect of the discount allowed.

(e) Explain the treatment of the totals of the discount columns in the cash book at the end of each month.

20. Sara started a business on 1 July 20-7. On that date she paid $20 000 into a business bank account. She decided to maintain a three column cash book and to divide her ledger into three sections – sales, purchases and nominal.

Sara's transactions for the first month of trading were as follows:

July   3 Withdrew $200 from the bank for office use
     5 Paid rent, $350, by cheque
     7 Purchased goods, $1500, on credit from BeeLine & Co
   10 Received long term loan, $6000, by cheque from HiFinance
   13 Bought motor vehicle, $5900, and paid by cheque
   17 Paid motor expenses, $150, in cash
   20 Sold goods, $2100, on credit to Honey Farm
   22 Paid BeeLine & Co a cheque to settle their account less 3% cash discount
   25 Honey Farm returned goods, $100
   28 Purchased goods, $930, on credit from BeeLine & Co
       Paid $20 in cash for carriage on purchases
   31 Received a cheque from Honey Farm for $1950 in full settlement of their account

(a) Enter the above transactions in the books of Sara. Balance the cash and bank columns in the cash book at 31 July and bring down the balances on 1 August.

(b) Transfer the totals of the discount columns to the relevant accounts in the nominal ledger.

(c) Balance the accounts in the sales and purchases ledgers as required.

(d) Draw up a trial balance at 31 July 20-7.

*21. Mirza is a trader. On 1 November 20-2 he had the following balances on his books.

	$
Cash book – cash	400 Dr
bank	5 900 Dr
Sales ledger – Redfern Traders	500
Purchases ledger – Square Tiles Co	2 300
Nominal ledger – capital	44 000
machinery	30 000
inventory	3 500
fixtures and fittings	6 000

Enter the above balances in the appropriate accounts on 1 November 20-2.

The following transactions took place during November 20-2.

November 3 Sold goods, $350, on credit to Southern Traders
7 Bought goods, $1600, on credit from Square Tiles Co
10 Received commission, $210, in cash
15 Returned goods, $230, to Square Tiles Co
17 Paid for machine repairs, $570, by cheque
18 Received a cheque, $500, from Redfern Traders
20 Paid a cheque to Square Tiles Co for the amount owing on 1 November less 2% cash discount
22 Received a cheque, $340, from Southern Traders in full settlement of the amount due
25 Cash sales, $1620
28 The bank returned Redfern Traders' cheque as dishonoured
30 Paid all the cash into the bank except $500

Enter the above transactions in the books of Mirza.

Balance the cash book and personal accounts as necessary on 30 November 20-2 and bring down the balances on 1 December 20-2. Transfer the totals of the discount columns to the nominal ledger on 30 November 20-2.

Draw up a trial balance on 30 November 20-2.

Chapter 5 Business Documents

22. Explain the purpose of a statement of account.
23. Neither the supplier nor the customer makes entries in their accounting records when a debit note is issued. Explain why.
24. Tracey is a credit customer of Lydia.

The following documents are issued in February 20-8: cheque; receipt; invoice; statement of account; debit note; credit note.

Complete the table below listing the documents in the order in which they would be issued. Name the person who would issue each document.

	Document in order of issue	Name of person issuing the document
(a)	....	....
(b)	....	....
(c)	....	....
(d)	....	....
(e)	....	....
(f)	....	....

42 *Cambridge O Level Principles of Accounts Workbook*

25. The following account appears in the ledger of Simon.

Paul account

Date	Details	Folio	$	Date	Details	Folio	$
20-6				20-6			
Jan 7	Purchases returns		120	Jan 4	Purchases		520
21	Bank		390				
	Discount		10				
			520				520

(a) Complete the following table by placing a tick (✓) against **each** document Simon would have used as a source of information in preparing the above account.

Document	✓
cheque	
credit note	
debit note	
invoice	
statement of account	

(b) Select **one** of the documents you have **not** ticked and explain why this was not used in the preparation of the ledger account.

26. Study the invoice shown below and answer the questions that follow.

Sales Invoice
Building Supplies
Lobastse Road
Francistown

Peter Onamusi
Mokolodi Road
Kgale   13 April 20-1

Quantity	Description	Price per unit $		Total $
25 metres	Floorboards	1.60 per metre		40.00
50 metres	Treated timber posts	2.20 per metre	(i)	
6	Doors	(ii)		300.00
			(iii)	
	Less 20% Trade discount		(iv)	
			(v)	

Terms: 2 ½% cash (vi) [＿＿＿＿] if paid within 30 days

(a) State the name of the business issuing the invoice.
(b) Calculate and write down the missing amounts at **(i)** to **(v)**.
(c) State the word which is missing at **(vi)**.
(d) Explain why the supplier has allowed the customer trade discount.
(e) State the amount of the cheque which was sent to pay for the goods on 4 May 20-1.
(f) Complete the following table to show how the invoice would be recorded in the books of both the supplier and the customer.

	Account to be debited	*Account to be credited*
(i) Supplier's books	....	....
(ii) Customer's books	....	....

*27. Study the business document shown below and answer the questions that follow.

(i) .... **Note**

Building Supplies
Lobastse Road
Francistown

James Moyo
Unit 2 Industrial Estate
Mahalapye   17 November 20-5

Quantity	Description	Unit price	Total $
40	Floor tiles Design XR234	$2	**(ii)**
	Less 25% Trade discount		**(iii)**
			(iv)
	Reason for return – Damage		

(a) State the word which is missing at **(i)**.
(b) Calculate and write down the missing amounts at **(ii)** to **(iv)**.
(c) Name the document which James Moyo may have sent to Building Supplies which resulted in the above document being issued.
(d) Explain why it is necessary to deduct trade discount on the above document.
(e) On 1 November 20-6 James Moyo owed Building Supplies $330. He purchased further goods, $280, on credit on 10 November. After the above document was issued on 17 November, there were no further transactions in November. James Moyo settled his account by cheque on 30 November after deducting a cash discount of 2%.

Prepare the account of James Moyo for November 20-6 as it would appear in the ledger of Building Supplies.

44 *Cambridge O Level Principles of Accounts Workbook*

(f)   (i) State the ledger of James Moyo in which the account of Building Supplies would appear.

(ii) State the ledger of Building Supplies in which the account of James Moyo would appear.

Chapter 6   Books of Prime Entry

28. List **five** books of original entry.
29. State **two** advantages of maintaining a sales journal.
30. During October, Susie listed her credit purchases in her purchases journal and totalled the journal at the end of the month. State what entries will be made in Susie's ledgers at the end of October.
31. Ben is a sole trader who buys and sells on credit. He maintains a full set of accounting records. He provided the following information for May 20-2.

Date	Transaction	Supplier	$
May 4	Goods bought	Pet Products Ltd	560
12	Goods bought	Cosy Canines	634
16	Goods returned	Cosy Canines	28
21	Goods bought	Pampered Pets & Co	422
27	Goods returned	Pampered Pets & Co	12

(a)   Enter the above transactions in Ben's purchases journal and purchases returns journal. Total the journals on 31 May 20-2.

(b)   Make the necessary entries in the following accounts in Ben's ledgers – purchases account, purchases returns account, Pet Products Ltd account, Cosy Canines account and Pampered Pets & Co account.

(c)   Complete the following table to indicate in which of Ben's ledgers **each** of the following accounts would appear.

Account	Ledger
Purchases account	....
Purchases returns account	....
Pet Products Ltd account	....
Cosy Canines account	....
Pampered Pets & Co account	....

*32. Nahida is a trader who keeps a full set of accounting records. Her transactions for June 20-9 included the following.

Sales Journal

20-9		$	$
June 10	London Road Stores		
	Goods		310
21	West End Fashions		
	Goods	350	
	Trade discount	<u>70</u>	<u>280</u>
30	Total for month		<u>590</u>

Structured Accounting Questions 45

Sales Returns Journal

20-9			$	$
June	27	West End Fashions		
		Goods	100	
		Trade discount	20	80
	30	Total for month		80

Cash Book (debit side)

			Discount Allowed	Cash	Bank
20-9			$	$	$
June	14	London Road Stores	6		234
	28	West End Fashions	5		195
	30	Sales		2120	

On 1 June there was a debit balance of $240 on London Road Stores' account.

(a) Write up the accounts of London Road Stores and West End Fashions as they would appear in Nahida's sales ledger for the month of June 20-9. Balance or total the accounts as necessary.

(b) Write up the sales account and the sales returns account as they would appear in Nahida's general ledger for the month of June 20-9.

(c) Complete the following table to show the business document and the book of prime entry which would be used for the following transactions.

Transaction	Document used by Nahida	Nahida's book of prime entry	Document used by Coco	Coco's book of prime entry
Goods sold on credit by Coco to Nahida	....	....	....	....
Goods returned by Nahida to Coco	....	....	....	....

Chapter 7 Financial Statements – Part A

33. (a) Explain the difference between gross profit and net profit.
(b) State how the cost of sales is calculated.

34. Complete the following table to show the double entry for transferring the following items to the income statement for the year ended 28 February 20-2.

	Debit	Credit
Total purchases	....	....
Total sales returns	....	....
Total general expenses	....	....
Total rent received	....	....
Inventory on 1 March 20-1	....	....

46   *Cambridge O Level Principles of Accounts Workbook*

*35. The following accounts appear in the ledger of Jane on 31 December 20-7.

Sales account

Date	Details	Folio	$	Date	Details	Folio	$
				20-7 Dec 31	Total for year		89 000

Wages and salaries account

Date	Details	Folio	$	Date	Details	Folio	$
20-7 Dec 31	Total paid		20 500				

Rent received account

Date	Details	Folio	$	Date	Details	Folio	$
				20-7 Dec 31	Total received		5200

Purchases returns account

Date	Details	Folio	$	Date	Details	Folio	$
				20-7 Dec 31	Total for year		490

Inventory account

Date	Details	Folio	$	Date	Details	Folio	$
20-7 Jan 1	Balance	b/d	4400				

Drawings account

Date	Details	Folio	$	Date	Details	Folio	$
20-7 Dec 31	Total for year		8000				

Capital account

Date	Details	Folio	$	Date	Details	Folio	$
				20-7 Jan 1	Balance	b/d	40 000

Close the above accounts at 31 December 20-7 as appropriate. The inventory on 31 December 20-7 was valued at $5300. The profit for the year ended 31 December 20-7 was $6000.

Structured Accounting Questions   47

36. Mustafa is a financial advisor. He provided the following information for the year ended 30 June 20-4.

	$
Commission received	84 000
Interest received	2 300
Rent and rates	12 000
General office expenses	8 050
Salary of assistant	25 000
Postages and telephone expenses	4 950

Prepare Mustafa's income statement for the year ended 30 June 20-4.

37. Haleema is a trader. She provided the following information for the year ended 31 August 20-3.

	$
Revenue (Sales)	80 000
Purchases	35 000
Sales returns	2 000
Carriage inwards	7 500
Carriage outwards	5 000
Inventory 1 September 20-2	10 000
Inventory 31 August 20-3	16 000
Discount allowed	450
Discount received	230
General expenses	18 000
Wages	24 000

Prepare Haleema's income statement for the year ended 31 August 20-3.

Chapter 8   Financial Statements – Part B

38. Lee Sang provided the following list of his assets and liabilities. Indicate with a tick (✓) the section of Lee Sang's balance sheet where each item would appear.

	Non-current assets	Current assets	Current liabilities	Non-current liabilities	Capital
Machinery					
Inventory					
Trade payables					
Trade receivables					
Drawings					
Cash					
Bank overdraft					
5 year bank loan					
Loss for the year					

48 *Cambridge O Level Principles of Accounts Workbook*

39. **(a)** State the order in which non-current assets are usually shown in a balance sheet. Use an example to illustrate your answer.
    (b) State the order in which current assets are usually shown in a balance sheet. Use an example to illustrate your answer.
    (c) State how net current assets is calculated.

40. The following balances remain on the books of Samira on 31 March 20-1 after the preparation of her income statement for the year ended 31 March 20-1.

	$
Capital 1 April 20-0	140 000
Premises	80 000
Inventory 31 March 20-1	12 000
Trade receivables	9 000
Trade payables	12 000
Fixtures and equipment	30 000
Drawings	9 000
Bank overdraft	4 700
Cash	200
Loan from AB Loans repayable 1 January 20-6	10 000
Motor vehicle	15 000
Loss for the year	11 500

Prepare Samira's balance sheet at 31 March 20-1.

41. Vijay is an IT consultant. His trial balance on 31 May 20-6 was as follows:

	Debit $		Credit $
Premises	50 000	Capital 1 June 20-5	80 000
Trade receivables	12 500	Trade payables	1 600
Office equipment	10 400	Fees received	136 000
Salaries	72 500	Rent received	10 000
Motor vehicle	9 300		
Motor vehicle expenses	1 480		
Bank	13 900		
Discount allowed	2 100		
Cash	100		
Office expenses	13 570		
Rates and insurance	6 750		
Drawings	35 000		
	227 600		227 600

Prepare Vijay's income statement for the year ended 31 May 20-6 and a balance sheet at 31 May 20-6.

*42. Bethany's trial balance at 31 July 20-9 was as follows:

	Debit $	Credit $
Capital 1 August 20-8		70 000
Drawings	4 100	
Premises	50 000	
Fixtures and fittings	10 600	
Office equipment	4 900	
Bank charges	300	
Lighting and heating	2 500	
Rates and insurance	5 100	
Repairs and maintenance	3 080	
General expenses	2 070	
Carriage inwards	7 500	
Carriage outwards	2 950	
Commission received		4 000
Revenue (Sales)		62 000
Purchases	36 000	
Sales returns	2 000	
Purchases returns		3 000
Inventory 1 June 20-8	7 000	
Bank	1 330	
Trade receivables	2 230	
Trade payables		2 660
	141 660	141 660

Inventory on 31 July 20-9 was valued at $6100.

Prepare Bethany's income statement for the year ended 31 July 20-9 and a balance sheet at 31 July 20-9.

Chapter 9   Accounting Rules

43. Explain what is meant by **each** of the following accounting principles. Use examples to illustrate your answer.
    (a) Business entity
    (b) Going concern
    (c) Accounting period
    (d) Historical cost

44. "It is important that financial statements can be understood by the users of those statements". State the accounting object being described.

45. Explain the accounting term "comparability".

46. The information provided in financial statements can be regarded as reliable if it is capable of being independently verified.

    State **two** other conditions which must be present for such information to be reliable.

50   *Cambridge O Level Principles of Accounts Workbook*

47. (a) State whether **each** of the following transactions represents capital expenditure, capital receipt, revenue expenditure or revenue receipt.

   (i) Purchase of machinery
   (ii) Purchase of goods for resale
   (iii) Commission received
   (iv) Proceeds of sale of machinery

   (b) Explain the effect on the profit for the year if $100 for the payment of motor vehicle expenses was included in the motor vehicles account.

48. (a) State two features of **each** of the following.

   (i) Capital expenditure
   (ii) Revenue expenditure

   (b) State whether **each** of the following payments represents capital expenditure or revenue expenditure.

   (i) Purchase price of premises
   (ii) Legal fees for the purchase of premises
   (iii) Insurance of premises
   (iv) Re-painting outside of premises
   (v) Installation of air conditioning in premises

*49. Ali is a trader. He has very little knowledge of accounting, but prepared the following statement at the end of his first year of trading on 31 January 20-7.

	$	$
Sale of goods	36 000	
Proceeds of sale of ¼ of equipment	1 000	37 000
Less Purchases of goods	18 000	
Purchases of equipment	4 000	
	22 000	
Less Closing inventory of goods	1 500	
	20 500	
General expenses	5 220	
Rent and rates	8 100	
Insurance	450	
Drawings from bank	10 000	44 270
Loss		7 270

   (a) Redraft the above statement, using a correct heading and correct format.
   (b) Select **two** of the items you have not included in your statement and explain why you have **not** included these items.

50. In connection with inventory, explain the difference between cost and net realisable value.

51. (a) State the basis on which inventory should be valued.
   (b) Name the principle which is being following if inventory is valued on the correct basis.
   (c) Explain the principle named in **(b)**.

*52. Martha is a trader. She provided the following information about her inventory at the end of her first year of trading.

Code number	Number of units	Cost price per unit $	Selling price per unit $
DZ22	410	21	18
LS15	290	15	22
SH49	300	25	36

The cost per unit of LS15 does not include carriage inwards of $2 per unit.

(a) Calculate the value of **each** type of inventory. Show your calculations.
(b) Explain the basis for your valuation in **each** case.
(c) Calculate the total value of inventory. Show your calculations.

Chapter 10   Other Payables and Other Receivables

53. Yee Song's payments for the year ended 31 December 20-8 included the following.

	$
Wages	68 000
Insurance (for 12 months to 30 June 20-9)	2 400

At 1 January 20-8 wages due amounted to $1300 and insurance prepaid amounted to $1140. At 31 December 20-8 wages due amounted to $1550.

Write up the wages account and the insurance account as they would appear in Yee Song's ledger for the year ended 31 December 20-8. Balance the accounts and show the amounts transferred to the income statement.

54. Zeema's financial year ends on 30 September. She sublets part of her premises to Faith at an annual rent of $6600.

On 1 October 20-3 Faith owed 1 month's rent. During the year ended 30 September 20-4 Faith paid rent of $8250.

(a) Write up Zeema's rent received account for the year ended 30 September 20-4. Balance the account and show the amount transferred to the income statement.
(b) Prepare a relevant extract from Zeema's income statement for the year ended 30 September 20-4.
(c) Prepare a relevant extract from Zeema's balance sheet at 30 September 20-4.

*55. Mandeep's financial year ends on 30 June.

(a) On 1 January 20-4, Mandeep sublet part of his premises to Mahender at an annual rent of $2600 payable quarterly in advance. Mahender gave Mandeep a cheque representing three month's rent on 1 January, 1 April and 30 June 20-4.

52   *Cambridge O Level Principles of Accounts Workbook*

Write up the rent received account as it would appear in Mandeep's ledger for the year ended 30 June 20-4. Balance the account and show the amount transferred to the income statement.

(b) Aneela pays Mandeep a commission on any goods purchased from her by Mandeep's customers. The commission is paid quarterly in arrears. During Mandeep's financial year ended 30 June 20-4 he received cheques for commission as follows:

	$
2 July 20-3	520
3 October 20-3	410
3 January 20-4	630
2 March 20-4	340

On 1 July 20-3 $520 commission was outstanding and on 30 June 20-4 $480 commission was outstanding.

Write up the commission received account as it would appear in Mandeep's ledger for the year ended 30 June 20-4. Balance the account and show the amount transferred to the income statement.

(c) State and explain the accounting principle which Mandeep is applying in his treatment of rent received and commission received.

56. Jane Banda is a trader. Her trial balance at 31 December 20-6 was as follows:

Debit	$	*Credit*	$
Drawings	17 000	Capital 1 January 20-6	110 000
Premises	80 000	Revenue (Sales)	350 000
Fixtures and fittings	14 000	Purchases returns	10 000
Motor vehicle	9 500	Discount received	4 100
Purchases	280 000	Rent received	5 500
Inventory 1 January 20-6	20 000	Trade payables	23 300
Carriage inwards	5 000	Bank overdraft	17 200
General expenses	12 200		
Rates and insurance	5 490		
Repairs and maintenance	3 870		
Salaries	41 000		
Motor vehicle expenses	2 940		
Trade receivables	29 100		
	520 100		520 100

The following additional information is available.

1   Inventory at 31 December 20-6 was valued at $24 000.
2   At 31 December 20-6 rent receivable due amounted to $500 and salaries due amounted to $3500.
3   Insurance, $2800, paid during the year was for 14 months to 28 February 20-6.

Structured Accounting Questions 53

4   Bank charges amounting to $790 had not been entered in the books.

Prepare Jane Banda's income statement for the year ended 31 December 20-6 and a balance sheet at that date.

*57. The following balance remained on the books of Leo Dlamini after the calculation of his gross profit for the year ended 31 October 20-7.

	$	$
Gross profit		34 500
Equipment	32 000	
Fixtures and fittings	13 600	
Capital 1 November 20-6		44 000
Drawings	5 000	
Stationery	380	
Wages	19 800	
Inventory 31 October 20-7	6 500	
Trade receivables	3 740	
Trade payables		3 500
Rent and rates	2 600	
Office expenses	3 100	
Heating and lighting	2 200	
Bank overdraft		2 120
Bank charges	200	
Loan from Finance Solutions Ltd		5 000
	89 120	89 120

The following additional information is available.

1   At 31 October 20-7 –   rates prepaid amounted to $220
wages outstanding amounted to $790
inventory of stationery was valued at $95

2   Leo Dlamini borrowed $5000 from Finance Solutions Ltd on 1 November 20-6. Interest is charged at the rate of 5% per annum.

(a)   Prepare Leo Dlamini's income statement for the year ended 31 October 20-7.

(b)   Prepare Leo Dlamini's balance sheet at 31 October 20-7.

Chapter 11   Depreciation and Disposal of Fixed Assets

58. Omar started business on 1 August 20-1. On that date he purchased machinery costing $20 000. He estimated that the machinery would last for 5 years when it would have a residual value of $2000. At the end of his financial year Omar was advised to depreciate his machinery.

(a)   Explain what is meant by depreciation.

(b)   State **two** causes of depreciation.

(c)   State **two** reasons why it is necessary to charge depreciation.

(d)   Name **two** accounting principles which are observed by charging depreciation.

54   *Cambridge O Level Principles of Accounts Workbook*

    (e) Calculate the deprecation charge for **each** of the three years ended 31 July 20-2, 20-3 and 20-4 using:

        (i) the straight line method of depreciation.

        (ii) the reducing balance method of depreciation at 40% per annum.

59. Gugu began business on 1 May 20-1. On that date she purchased equipment, $30 000, on credit from Superquip. She decided to use the straight line method of depreciation at the rate of 20% per annum, calculated from the date of purchase.

On 1 November 20-2 Gugu purchased additional equipment, $10 000, and paid by cheque.

(a) Write up the equipment account and the provision for depreciation of equipment account in Gugu's ledger for the two years ended 30 April 20-2 and 30 April 20-3.

(b) Prepare a relevant extract from Gugu's income statement for the year ended 30 April 20-3.

(c) Prepare a relevant extract from Gugu's balance sheet at 30 April 20-3.

60. Dinesh started business on 1 January 20-3 on which date he bought two machines costing $9000 each. He decided to depreciate the machines using the straight line method at 20% per annum, calculated on the cost of machines held at the end of each financial year.

On 30 June 20-6 Dinesh sold one machine for $2800 which he received in cash.

On 1 July 20-6 Dinesh purchased a new machine, $12 000, on credit from Western Ltd

(a)   **(i)** Calculate the cost of machinery held on 1 January 20-6. Enter this as a balance in the machinery account.

        (ii) Calculate the total depreciation up to 1 January 20-6. Enter this as a balance in the provision for depreciation of machinery account.

(b) Make the necessary entries in the nominal ledger account of Dinesh for the year ended 31 December 20-6. Balance the accounts as necessary.

*61. (a) Explain how depreciation is an example of the application of the principle of matching **and** the principle of prudence.

(b) Explain why it is important that the same method of depreciation is used each year for the same type of asset.

(c) Melody started business on 1 October 20-4. On that date she purchased equipment, $10 000, on credit from Superquip. Melody decided to depreciate equipment using the straight line method at 20% per annum calculated on the cost of assets held at the end of each financial year.

On 1 October 20-5 Melody purchased additional equipment, $4000, paying by cheque. On 31 March 20-7 Melody sold half of the original equipment (purchased on 1 October 20-4) for $1800, cash.

        (i) Write up the equipment account, provision for depreciation of equipment account and equipment disposal account for the three years ended 30 September 20-5, 20-6 and 20-7.

Structured Accounting Questions 55

    (ii) Prepare a relevant extract from Melody's income statement for the year ended 30 September 20-7.
    (iii) Prepare a relevant extract from Melody's balance sheet at 30 September 20-7.

62. Dave Utaka is a business consultant. His trial balance at 31 July 20-9 was as follows:

	$	$
Capital 1 August 20-8		68 000
Drawings	18 600	
Premises at cost	55 000	
Fixtures and fittings at cost	9 500	
Motor vehicles at cost	28 000	
Provision for depreciation of fixtures and fittings		950
Provision for depreciation of motor vehicles		5 600
Long term loan from QT Ltd		10 000
Fees		102 000
General expenses	11 550	
Rates and insurance	11 400	
Wages and salaries	42 500	
Motor expenses	3 650	
Loan interest	300	
Trade receivables	7 800	
Trade payables		590
Bank overdraft		1 160
	188 300	188 300

Dave Utaka provided the following additional information.

1   At 31 July 20-9 rates and insurance prepaid amounted to $320.
2   A bank statement received on 31 July 20-9 showed bank charges, $140. This had not been recorded in the accounting records.
3   The loan from QT Ltd was received on 1 August 20-8. Interest is charged at the rate of 6% per annum.
4   Depreciation is charged on the fixtures and fittings at 10% per annum using the straight line method and at 20% per annum on the motor vehicles using the reducing balance method.

(a) Prepare Dave Utaka's income statement for the year ended 31 July 20-9.
(b) Prepare Dave Utaka's balance sheet at 31 July 20-9.

*63. Varsha Rahman is a trader. She provided the following trial balance at 31 December 20-0.

	$	$
Purchases	120 000	
Revenue (Sales)		190 000
Inventory 1 January 20-0	7 000	
Premises at cost	40 000	
Equipment at cost	19 000	
Provision for depreciation of equipment		5 700
Motor vehicles	12 000	

(Continued)

56 Cambridge O Level Principles of Accounts Workbook

Provision for depreciation of motor vehicles		4 320
General expenses	21 200	
Wages	31 750	
Rates and insurance	9 200	
Loan interest	90	
Commission received		4 000
Discount received		1 950
Trade receivables	14 400	
Trade payables		8 940
Bank	5 790	
Capital 1 January 20-0		68 000
Drawings	8 480	
Long term loan – A1 Finance		6 000
	288 910	288 910

Varsha Rahman supplied the following additional information.

1   Inventory at 31 December 20-0 was valued at $8500.
2   At 31 December 20-0 commission receivable due amounted to $200 and wages due amounted to $2140.
3   The amount paid for rates, $4800, is for 15 months to 31 March 20-1.
4   During the year ended 31 December 20-0 Varsha took goods costing $940 for her own use.
    This has not been entered in the accounting records.
5   The loan from A1 Finance was obtained on 1 July 20-0 and interest is charged at 6% per annum.
6   Depreciation on equipment is charged at 10% per annum using the straight line method and depreciation on motor vehicles is charged at 20% per annum using the reducing balance method.

(a) Prepare the income statement of Varsha Rahman for the year ended 31 December 20-0.
(b) Prepare the balance sheet of Varsha Rahman at 31 December 20-0.

Chapter 12   Bad Debts and Provisions for Doubtful Debts

64. Waqas is a trader. His financial year ends on 31 August. He provided the following information.

	$
31 August 20-2 Trade receivables	5500
31 August 20-3 Trade receivables	6200
31 August 20-4 Trade receivables	4900

On 31 August 20-2 a provision for doubtful debts was created. Waqas decided that it would be maintained at 3% of the trade receivables at the end of each financial year.

(a) Write up the provision for doubtful debts account as it would appear in the ledger of Waqas for the three years ended 31 August 20-2, 31 August 20-3 and 31 August 20-4.

(b) Prepare a relevant extract from the balance sheet of Waqas at 31 August 20-2, 31 August 20-3 and 31 August 20-4.

65. Hiba's financial year ends on 31 October. Hiba's trade receivables amounted to $34 250 on 28 October 20-7. This included the following amounts which had been outstanding for over two years.

	$
J Mavuso	480
K Ngwenga	1520
L Makamba	250

On 30 October 20-7

1   Hiba decided to write off L Makamba's debt as irrecoverable.
2   J Mavuso sent a cheque for $450 and a letter to say he was unable to pay the balance. Hiba wrote off the balance as a bad debt.
3   A letter was received stating that K Ngwenga was bankrupt. A cheque was enclosed for a first and final dividend of 70c in the $. Hiba wrote off the remaining balance as a bad debt.

On 31 October Hiba decided to create a provision for doubtful debts of 2 ½% of the remaining trade receivables.

Write up the following accounts in Hiba's ledger.

(a) J Mavuso account
(b) K Ngwenga account
(c) L Makamba account
(d) Bad debts account
(e) Provision for doubtful debts account

66. The following accounts appear in the ledger of Sanath whose financial year ends on 30 June.

Bad debts account

Date	Details	Folio	$	Date	Details	Folio	$
20-4				20-5			
Oct 1	PK Stores		200	Jun 30	Income statement		450
20-5							
May 1	Sellfast & Co		250				
			450				450

Provision for doubtful debts account

Date	Details	Folio	$	Date	Details	Folio	$
20-5				20-4			
June 30	Income statement			July 1	Balance	b/d	700
			100				
	Balance	c/d	600				
			700				700
				20-5			
				July 1	Balance	b/d	600

58　*Cambridge O Level Principles of Accounts Workbook*

Explain **each** entry in the above accounts and also state where the double entry for **each** entry will be found.

*67. Alice's financial year ends on 30 November. On 1 December 20-3 the balance on her provision for doubtful debts account was $500. On 1 November 20-4 Alice's debtors included Safat Stores who owed $590 and El Nil Traders who owed $1400.

Alice's transactions for the month ended 30 November 2004 included the following.

November 5	Received a cheque from El Nil Traders in settlement of their account less a 2% cash discount
14	Sold goods, $420, on credit to El Nil Traders
27	Received a cheque, $490, for a final settlement of Safat Stores who were bankrupt. Alice wrote off the remaining balance as a bad debt
30	Alice decided to maintain her provision for doubtful debts at 4% of the trade receivables who owed $13 500 on that date

(a) Write up the following accounts in Alice's ledger.
  (i) Safat Stores account
  (ii) El Nil Traders account
  (iii) Bad debts account
  (iv) Provision for doubtful debts account
(b) Prepare a relevant extract from Alice's income statement for the year ended 30 November 20-4.
(c) Prepare a relevant extract from Alice's balance sheet at 30 November 20-4.
(d) State and explain one accounting principle Alice is applying by maintaining a provision for doubtful debts.

68. Thabo Manana owns a gardening and home services business. He provided the following trial balance on 28 February 20-7.

	Debit		Credit
	$		$
Drawings	9 200	Capital 1 March 20-6	30 000
Bank	1 040	Trade payables	750
Trade receivables	4 300	Provision for doubtful debts	200
Equipment at valuation	10 860	Income from customers	42 000
Motor vehicles at valuation	16 000	Commission received	2 420
Motor expenses	2 850		
Insurance	1 970		
Repairs & maintenance	2 590		
Wages	26 100		
Bad debts	150		
General expenses	310		
	75 370		75 370

The following additional information is available.
1 General expenses owing 28 February 20-7 amounted to $43.
2 Motor expenses includes motor insurance, $806, for 13 months to 31 March 20-7.

3 The provision for doubtful debts is maintained at 5% of the trade receivables at the end of each financial year.

4 The non-current assets are depreciated using the revaluation method. On 28 February 20-7 the equipment was valued at $10 120 and the motor vehicles were valued at $13 850.

Prepare Thabo Manana's income statement for the year ended 28 February 20-7 and a balance sheet at 28 February 20-7.

69. Katie Womba is a trader. The following is her trial balance at 31 May 20-9 after the calculation of her gross profit.

	Debit		Credit
	$		$
Rent	13 100	Gross profit	140 000
Rates and insurance	8 100	Discount received	3 200
Wages	79 500	Provision for depreciation	
Office expenses	2 100	of fixtures & fittings	7 410
General expenses	6 300	Provision for depreciation	
Fixtures & fittings at cost	39 000	of motor vehicles	6 480
Motor vehicles at cost	18 000	Trade payables	31 500
Inventory 31 May 20-9	39 050	Provision for doubtful debts	850
Trade receivables	24 300	Capital 1 June 20-8	70 000
Bank	12 190		
Drawings	17 800		
	259 440		259 440

Katie Womba provided the following additional information.

1 The general expenses include telephone expenses. At 31 May 20-9 a telephone account of $80 was unpaid.

2 The office expenses include office stationery. At 31 May 20-9 the inventory of stationery was valued at $122.

3 A debtor owing $100 should be written off as a bad debt.

4 The provision for doubtful debts should be adjusted to equal 3% of the remaining trade receivables.

5 The non-current assets are depreciated using the reducing balance method at the rate of 10% per annum for the fixtures and fittings and 20% per annum for the motor vehicles.

(a) Prepare Katie Womba's income statement for the year ended 31 May 20-9.

(b) Prepare Katie Womba's balance sheet at 31 May 20-9.

70. Tahir is a trader. His financial year ends on 31 May. After the preparation of the trading account section of the income statement for the year ended 31 May 20-4 the following balances remained on his books.

	$
Gross profit	42 000
Premises at cost	60 000
Fixtures and equipment at cost	22 000
Motor vehicles at cost	18 000

(Continued)

60 *Cambridge O Level Principles of Accounts Workbook*

Trade receivables	9 900
Trade payables	7 480
General expenses	4 950
Motor expenses	3 260
Provision for doubtful debts	420
Bad debts	270
Commission receivable	2 800
6% Loan (repayable in 15 years)	10 000
Wages	22 400
Rates and insurance	4 300
Provision for depreciation of fixtures and equipment	6 600
Provision for depreciation of motor vehicles	6 480
Inventory 31 May 20-4	8 200
Capital 1 June 20-3	86 500
Drawings	5 500
Bank	3 200 Dr

The following additional information is available.
1   At 31 May 20-4
    Commission receivable outstanding amounted to $160
    6 months loan interest is outstanding
    The rates and insurance amount of $4200 includes $1800 insurance which
    represents 18 months' insurance to 30 November 20-4
2   The provision for doubtful debts is to be maintained at 4% of the trade
    receivables.
3   The fixtures and equipment is being depreciated at 15% per annum using
    the straight line method.
4   The motor vehicles are being depreciated at 20% per annum using the
    reducing balance method.
    (a) Prepare the income statement of Tahir for the year ended 31 May 20-4.
    (b) Prepare the balance sheet of Tahir at 31 May 20-4.

Chapter 13   Bank Reconciliation Statements

71. The pages of Dwight's cash book relating to June 20-0 were damaged when a
bottle of ink was spilt. He obtained a copy of his bank statement which showed
a positive bank balance of $3540 on 30 June.

Comparing the bank statement with his paying-in book and cheque book,
Dwight found that –

1   Cheques sent to the following creditors had not been presented for
    payment

	$
Beach Street Stores	295
Jamaica Road Boutique	182
Kingston Kids Ltd	304

Structured Accounting Questions 61

2 The following amounts paid into the bank on 29 June had not been credited by the bank –

	$
Cash sales	935
Cheques received from Hi-Fashion Ltd	242
Bermuda Road Boutique	187

Calculate the balance which appeared in the bank column of Dwight's cash book on 30 June 20-0. Show your calculations.

72. Christina balanced her cash book on 31 October 20-4 and brought down a debit balance of $3280 on 1 November. Her bank statement for October 20-4 showed a closing credit balance of $208.

When comparing the cash book with the bank statement, Christina found that–

1 The following items appeared only in the cash book –
Cheque, $280, paid to Wilma, a creditor
Cash sales $1643

2 The following items appeared only on the bank statement –
Bank charges of $109
Insurance, $850, paid by standing order

3 The bank had debited Christina's business bank account with a standing order for $750, for a life insurance policy premium which should have been paid from Christina's personal bank account.

(a) Make any additional entries required in Christina's cash book. Calculate a new bank balance at 31 October 20-4. Bring down the balance on 1 November 20-4.

(b) Prepare a bank reconciliation statement at 31 October 20-4.

(c) State the bank balance that should be shown in Christina's balance sheet on 31 October 20-4 and state whether it is an asset or a liability.

73. Raminder is a trader. All his sales and purchases are on credit terms, the accounts being settled by cheque. All expenses are paid by cheque.

Raminder's transactions for January 20-7 included the following.

		$
January	4 Cheque received from Aswan	2400
	10 Cheque paid to Ali (Cheque number 12456)	950
	17 Cheque paid to Hassan (Cheque number 12457)	3050
	22 Cheque paid for rates (Cheque number 12458)	685
	29 Cheque paid for wages (Cheque number 12459)	1550
	30 Cheque received from Ahmed	784

Raminder had a debit balance of $8280 in his bank column in his cash book on 1 January 20-7.
Raminder received the following bank statement from his bank.

62   *Cambridge O Level Principles of Accounts Workbook*

	THE NEW BANK LTD **ANYTOWN**				
Customer: Raminder Singh			**Account No: 567443** **Date: 31 January 20-7**		
Date	*Details*		*Debit*	*Credit*	*Balance*
20-7			$	$	$
January 1	Balance				8 280 Cr
8	Credit No. 9985			2 400	10 680 Cr
15	Cheque No. 12456		950		9 730 Cr
18	Cheque No. 12457		3 050		6 680 Cr
26	Cheque No. 12458		685		5 995 Cr
30	SO Landlords Ltd (rent)		450		5 545 Cr
31	Bank charges		110		5 435 Cr

(a) Write up the bank columns in Raminder's cash book for January 20-7. Make any adjustments which are necessary after receiving the bank statement. Balance the cash book and bring down the balance on 1 February 20-7.

(b) Prepare Raminder's bank reconciliation statement at 31 January 20-7.

(c) Explain the meaning of **each** of the following terms used in connection with bank reconciliation.

  (i) unpresented cheques

  (ii) amounts not credited

*74. Wendy Li is a trader.

(a) State and explain **two** reasons why she should reconcile the balance on her bank statement with that shown in her cash book.

(b) Explain why items are recorded on the opposite side of a cash book to that on which they appear on a bank statement.

Wendy Li's cash book (bank columns) showed the following entries for September 20-8.

Cash Book (bank columns only)							
Date	*Details*	*Folio*	*$*	*Date*	*Details*	*Folio*	*$*
20-8				20-8			
Sept 1	Balance		310	Sept 12	Cheung Ltd		1750
8	East & West		290	18	W Tong & Co		1300
14	Chan & Co		1070				
29	J Tan		95				
30	Cash sales		1020				
	Balance	c/d	265				
			3050				3050
				20-8			
				Oct 1	Balance	b/d	265

The following bank statement was received by Wendy Li.

	THE NEW BANK LTD ANYTOWN			
Customer: Wendy Li			Account No: 679834 Date: 30 September 20-8	

Date	Details	Debit	Credit	Balance
20-8		$	$	$
Sept 1	Balance			440 Cr
4	Cheque No. 23457	130		310 Cr
13	Credit No. 3466		290	600 Cr
16	Cheque No. 23458	1750		1150 Dr
18	SO Insurance Co	195		1345 Dr
22	Credit No. 3467		1070	275 Dr
23	AB Ltd – Dividend received		204	71 Dr
30	Dishonoured cheque	290		361 Dr
	Charges	188		549 Dr

(c) Explain why the balance on Wendy Li's cash book on 1 September was not the same as the balance on the bank statement on that date.

(d) Make any additional entries that are required in the cash book of Wendy Li. Calculate a new bank balance at 30 September 20-8. Bring down the balance on 1 October 20-8.

(e) Prepare a bank reconciliation statement at 30 September 20-8.

Chapter 14 Journal Entries and Correction of Errors

75. Ben started a business on 1 May 20-2. He introduced the following into the business.

	$
Premises	85 000
Fixtures and fittings	18 000
Motor vehicle	11 500
Inventory	9 420

He also introduced $5300 in cash, $5100 of which was paid into a business bank account. Ben's father also paid $20 000 into the business bank account as a loan to the business.

(a) Prepare an opening journal entry for Ben on 1 May 20-2. A narrative is required.

(b) List **three** uses of a journal excluding opening entries.

(c) Explain why the journal is not part of the double entry system.

76. Melissa's financial year ends on 30 November.

On 30 November 20-5 Melissa's ledger accounts included the following.

	$
Sales for the year	74 300
Rates, including a prepayment of $40	1 080
Inventory 1 December 20-4	4 650

64 *Cambridge O Level Principles of Accounts Workbook*

On 30 November 20-5 –

1 Melissa discovered that no entry had been made to record the purchase of equipment, $5200, on credit from Superquip Ltd
2 $56 owing by a debtor, Roddy, should be written off as a bad debt
3 Inventory was valued at $5110
4 Equipment should be depreciated by $790

Prepare journal entries to record the above transactions, including transfers to the income statement. Narratives are required.

77. Sabeena is a trader. Her financial year ends on 31 January.

(a) On 31 January 20-9 the balances in Sabeena's ledger included the following:

	$
Purchases account	33 100
Sales returns account	1 290
Discount received	870

Prepare journal entries to transfer these balances to the income statement for the year ended 31 January 20-9. Narratives are **not** required.

(b) On 31 January 20-9 Sabeena's general expenses account had a debit balance of $1100.

This included $1000 business expenses, of which $90 was prepaid for the following financial year. The remainder was Sabeena's personal expenses.

Prepare journal entries to make the necessary year-end transfers from the general expenses account. Narratives are **not** required.

(c) On 31 January 20-9 Sabeena sold her motor vehicle on credit to Scrappers Ltd for $4000.

The motor vehicle had cost $10 500 and the depreciation to date amounted to $5124.

Prepare entries in Sabeena's journal to record the disposal of the motor vehicle. Narratives are **not** required.

(d) On 31 January 20-9 Sabeena's trade receivables amounted to $12 140. Her provision for doubtful debts was $400. The bad debts written off during the year amounted to $271.

On 31 January 20-9 Sabeena decided to write off $140 owed by Raj (included in the total trade receivables) and to adjust the provision for doubtful debts so that it equalled 4% of the remaining trade receivables.

Prepare journal entries to record the writing off of the bad debt, the adjustment of the provision for doubtful debts and year-end transfers to the income statement. Narratives are **not** required.

Structured Accounting Questions   65

78. Yee Sang's financial year ends on 31 August. The trial balance prepared on 31 August 20-0 showed a shortage on the credit side of $263. Yee Sang entered this in a suspense account.

The following errors were later discovered.

1   No entry had been made for goods costing $220 taken by Yee Sang for personal use.

2   $679 paid to Kuso, a creditor, had been recorded in his account as $697.

3   Motor vehicle expenses, $199, had been debited to the motor vehicles account.

4   Rent received from a tenant, $180, had been debited to the rent payable account.

5   No entry had been made in the ledger for office expenses, $15, paid in cash.

6   The sales returns journal was undercast by $100.

(a) Prepare the entries in Yee Sang's journal to correct the above errors. Narratives are required.

(b) Prepare the suspense account in Yee Sang's ledger to show the required amendments. Start with the balance arising from the difference on the trial balance.

(c) Explain why not all of the corrections require an entry in the suspense account. Illustrate your answer with an example from the above information.

*79. A trial balance prepared for Nyasha on 30 June 20-6 failed to balance. The debit side totalled $167 680 and the credit side totalled $167 934. Nyasha entered the difference in a suspense account and prepared a draft income statement which showed a profit for the year of $21 410.

The following errors were later discovered.

1   The purchases journal had been overcast by $100.

2   $285 received from J Khan had been entered in the account of K Khan, another debtor, in the sales ledger.

3   Goods, $95, returned to a supplier, Begum Stores, had been correctly recorded in the purchases returns journal, but had been credited to the account of Begum Stores.

4   A cheque, $74, for electricity had been correctly recorded in the bank account, but no other entry had been made.

5   Discount allowed, $90, had been omitted from the trial balance.

(a) Prepare the entries in Nyasha's journal to correct the above errors. Narratives are **not** required.

(b) Prepare the suspense account in Nyasha's ledger to show the necessary amendments. Start with the balance arising from the difference on the trial balance.

66   *Cambridge O Level Principles of Accounts Workbook*

(c) Using your answer to **(b)**, state whether you consider that all the errors in Nyasha's books have been discovered. Give a reason for your answer.

(d) Prepare a statement to show the corrected profit for the year ended 30 June 20-6.

80. Osama is a trader. He has only a limited knowledge of bookkeeping, but attempted to prepare a set of financial statements at the end of his first financial year on 31 December 20-5. The balance sheet he prepared is shown below.

	$
Non-current assets at cost	17 500
Inventory	1 830
Trade receivables	2 650
Drawings	5 100
	27 080
Capital at 1 January 20-5	21 000
Profit for the year	1 710
Trade payables	3 100
Bank overdraft	790
	26 600
Suspense account	480
	27 080

When the books were checked the following errors were discovered.

1 The non-current assets should have been depreciated by 10% on cost.

2 The sales account had been undercast by $500.

3 No adjustment had been made for rates and insurance, $40, paid in advance.

4 No entry had been made for goods costing $280 taken by Osama for personal use.

5 The bank statement on 31 December 20-5 showed bank charges of $81. No entry had been made in Osama's books.

6 A provision for doubtful debts of 2% of the trade receivables should have been made.

7 Office expenses, $20, have been correctly recorded in the bank account, but no other entry has been made.

(a) Prepare a statement to show Osama's corrected profit for the year ended 31 December 20-5.

(b) Prepare a corrected balance sheet of Osama at 31 December 20-5. Use a suitable form of presentation.

Structured Accounting Questions 67

Chapter 15 Control Accounts

81. Safiya maintains a full set of accounting records and prepares control accounts at the end of each month.
She provided the following information.

20-5			$
July	1	Purchases ledger control account balance	1740 credit
		Purchases ledger control account balance	20 debit
July	31	Totals for the month	
		Purchases journal	1860
		Purchases returns journal	29
		Cheques paid to creditors	1617
		Discounts received from creditors	33
		Interest charged by creditor on overdue account	15
		Contra item transferred from the sales ledger to the purchases ledger	90

(a) Prepare Safiya's purchases ledger control account for the month of July 20-5. There is only one balance on the account at the end of the month.

(b) State where Safiya obtained the relevant figure for **each** of the following items.

(i) Cheques paid to creditors

(ii) Discounts received

(iii) Contra item

(c) Explain how the contra item may have arisen.

82. The following information was obtained from the books of Marvan.

20-9		$
Mar 1	Balance brought down on sales ledger control account	4520 debit
	Totals of journals for March 20-9 were:	
	Sales	5180
	Sales returns	210
	The cash book for March 20-9 showed:	
	Cheques received from debtors	3977
	Discounts allowed to debtors	123
	The journal entries included the following:	
	Bad debt written off	58
	Inter ledger transfer	45
	Interest charged on overdue debtor's account	10
Mar 31	Sales ledger credit balances	90

(a) Prepare Marvan's sales ledger control account for the month ended 31 March 20-9.

(b) Explain **two** reasons why Marvan should prepare a sales ledger control account.

(c) State **two** reasons which may have resulted in a credit balance on a debtor's account.

(d) Calculate the rate of cash discount Marvan allowed to his debtors.

68　*Cambridge O Level Principles of Accounts Workbook*

83. Jaswant is a trader. She maintains a full set of accounting records and provided the following information for the month of February 20-8.

			$
Feb	1	Amount owing to credit suppliers	3490
		Amount owing by credit customers	4830
Feb	28	Goods sold on credit	5810
		Goods purchased on credit	3920
		Goods returned to credit suppliers	42
		Goods returned by credit customers	64
		Cheques received from credit customers	4365
		Cheques paid to credit suppliers	2925
		Discounts allowed	135
		Discounts received	75
		Balance in sales ledger transferred to purchases ledger	212
		Debit balance on creditor's account	46
		Credit balance on debtor's account	101

(a) Select the relevant figures and prepare Jaswant's purchases ledger control account for the month ended 28 February 20-8.

(b) The total of the credit balances in the purchases ledger on 28 February 20-8 did not agree with the credit balance on the purchases ledger control account. Explain the significance of this.

(c) Explain why Jaswant writes up her purchases ledger control account from the books of original entry and not from her purchases ledger.

*84. Sourav maintains a full set of accounting records and prepares control accounts at the end of each month.

(a) State **three** advantages of preparing control accounts.

(b) State **three** sources of information for the items in a sales ledger control account.

Sourav provided the following information at 31 July 20-3.

			$
July	1	Amount owing by credit customers	19 760
		Provision for doubtful debts	990
		Credit balance on credit customer's account	344
July	31	Totals for month:	
		Cash sales	14 350
		Credit sales	24 145
		Cheques received from credit customers	18 870
		Cheque received (included in the above figure)	
		later dishonoured	460
		Discount allowed	370
		Discount received	615
		Bad debts written off	175
		Returns by credit customers	738
		Sales ledger balances transferred to purchases ledger	242
		Credit balance on credit customer's account	196

Structured Accounting Questions   69

(c) Select the relevant figures and prepare Sourav's sales ledger control account for the month ended 31 July 20-3.

(d) Select **two** items listed above that should not be included in the sales ledger control account and explain why they do not appear.

Chapter 16   Incomplete Records

85. (a) Explain the meaning of **each** of the following terms.
    (i) Margin
    (ii) Mark up

    (b) At the end of her second year of trading Ansie provided the following information.

	$
Revenue (Sales)	40 200
Purchases	31 600
Sales returns	200
Purchases returns	400
Inventory 1 August 20-8	2 300

Ansie omitted to calculate the value of her inventory on 31 July 20-9 and did not maintain any inventory records during the year. She sells all goods at a profit margin of 25%.

Calculate, by means of a trading account section of an income statement, the value of Ansie's inventory on 31 July 20-9.

86. Some of Govinder's accounting records were badly damaged when his premises were flooded.

He was able to provide the following information.

Inventory 1 January 20-1	$3000
Inventory 31 December 20-1	$4000
Rate of inventory turnover	13.5 times
Mark up	20%

Prepare a detailed trading account section of an income statement for the year ended 31 December 20-1.

87. Belinda runs a secretarial agency. She does not maintain many accounting records.

On 1 September 20-5 she provided the following information.

	$
Premises at cost	80 000
Fixtures and equipment at cost	6 000
Motor vehicle at cost	11 800
Trade receivables	4 100
Wages accrued	600
Balance at bank	2 500
Long term loan – HiFinance Ltd	20 000

70   *Cambridge O Level Principles of Accounts Workbook*

During the year ended 31 August 20-6 Belinda paid off half of the long term loan. She purchased new equipment costing $1000 and withdrew $4500 from the bank for personal use.

At 31 August 20-6, the fixtures and equipment and motor vehicle should be depreciated by 20% on the cost of the assets held on that date.

On 31 August 20-6, wages accrued amounted to $570, trade receivables amounted to $4750 and there was a bank overdraft of $1420.

(a) Prepare a statement of affairs of Belinda at 1 September 20-5 showing the total capital at that date.

(b) Prepare a statement of affairs of Belinda at 31 August 20-6 showing the total capital at that date.

(c) Prepare a statement to show the calculation of Belinda's profit or loss for the year ended 31 August 20-6.

*88. Nabil is a trader. He has not kept a full set of accounting records, but was able to provide the following information.

	1 April 20-7 $	31 March 20-8 $
Inventory	5 300	6 050
Trade receivables	4 150	4 970
Trade payables	3 950	4 080
Machinery at cost	38 000	38 000
Equipment at cost	13 500	13 500
Motor vehicle at cost	9 400	9 400
Cash	100	100
Balance at bank	1 580	–
Bank overdraft	–	5 864
Other receivables	240	–
Other payables	120	170
Long term loan from El Tahrir Loans	15 000	5 000

At 31 March 20-8 Nabil decided that the machinery should be depreciated by 20% on cost and the equipment should be depreciated by 15% on cost. At that date the motor vehicle was revalued at $8100.

On 31 March 20-8 a debt of $170 should be written off as a bad debt. Nabil decided to create a provision for doubtful debts of 2% of the remaining trade receivables.

(a) Prepare a statement of affairs of Nabil at 1 April 20-7 showing his total capital at that date.

(b) Prepare a statement of affairs of Nabil at 31 March 20-8 showing his total capital at that date.

During the year ended 31 March 20-8 Nabil introduced a further $10 000 as capital. His drawings during the same period were $4400 in cash and goods costing $685.

(c) Prepare a statement showing the calculation of the profit or loss for the year for Nabil for the year ended 31 March 20-8.

Structured Accounting Questions 71

89. Chi Chi is a trader. Her financial year ends on 31 October. She provided the following information.

	1 November 20-4 $	31 October 20-5 $
Inventory	3870	3100
Trade receivables	4970	5250
Trade payables	6250	6950

During the year ended 31 October 20-5 –

	$
Cheques paid to credit suppliers	43 290
Cheques received from credit customers	43 120
Discounts received	1 110
Discounts allowed	880
Cash sales	15 720
Cash purchases	330

(a) Calculate Chi Chi's credit sales for the year ended 31 October 20-5 by means of a total trade receivables account.

(b) Calculate Chi Chi's credit purchases for the year ended 31 October 20-5 by means of a total trade payables account.

(c) Prepare the trading account section of Chi Chi's income statement for the year ended 31 October 20-5.

(d) Calculate Chi Chi's rate of inventory turnover for the year ended 31 October 20-5.

90. Balbir started a business on 1 May 20-4. He introduced capital of $80 000. This included premises, $50 000, machinery $14 000, and the remainder was deposited into a business bank account.

Balbir had only limited knowledge of bookkeeping and he did not maintain a full set of accounting records.

All purchases and sales were made on credit terms. Cheques received from debtors were banked on the day of receipt. Creditors and all expenses (other payables) were paid by cheque.

During the year ended 30 April 20-5 –

Receipts	$	Payments by cheque	$
Cheques from debtors	68 385	Creditors	57 915
		General expenses	160
		Machinery repairs	120
		Wages	6 556
		Rates & insurance	930
		Drawings	9 850

(a) Prepare a summarised bank account for the year ended 30 April 20-5. Balance the account and bring down the balance on 1 May 20-5.

During the year ended 30 April 20-5 Balbir returned goods, $150, to creditors. Discounts of $1485 were received from creditors. At 30 April 20-5, $17 650 was owed to credit suppliers.

72   *Cambridge O Level Principles of Accounts Workbook*

(b) Calculate, by means of a total trade payables account, the purchases for the year ended 30 April 20-5.

Sales during the year ended 30 April 20-5 amounted to $83 000 and sales returns amounted to $970. Discounts allowed to debtors totalled $2115. At 30 April 20-5 a bad debt, $230, should be written off.

(c) Calculate, by means of a total trade receivables account, the amount owed by credit customers on 30 April 20-5.

During the year ended 30 April 20-5, Balbir took goods costing $1550 for his own use.

Balbir did not value his inventory on 30 April 20-5.

All goods were sold at a margin of 20%.

(d) Prepare a detailed trading account section of the income statement of Balbir for the year ended 30 April 20-5, showing the value of the inventory on 30 April 20-5.

At 30 April 20-5 it was decided that the machinery should be depreciated by 10% on cost.

(e) Starting with the gross profit calculated in **(d)**, prepare a statement to show the calculation of the profit for the year for Balbir for the year ended 30 April 20-5.

(f) Prepare Balbir's balance sheet at 30 April 20-5.

Chapter 17   Accounts of Clubs and Societies

91. The treasurer of the Zabeel Social Club provided the following information for the year ended 31 December 20-2.

	$
Subscriptions received for the year ended 31 December 20-1	40
for the year ended 31 December 20-2	1800
for the year ending 31 December 20-3	60
Clubhouse rent paid for the year ended 31 December 20-2	780
for the year ending 31 December 20-3	45
Insurance paid for the year ended 31 December 20-2	320
General expenses paid for the year ended 31 December 20-2	515
Cost of new furniture	1100

On 1 January 20-2 there was a debit balance of $420 on the receipts and payments account.

(a) Prepare the receipts and payments account of the Zabeel Social Club for the year ended 31 December 20-2.

(b) State **two** differences between a receipts and payments account and an income and expenditure account.

Structured Accounting Questions 73

(c) Explain your reason for the figure you inserted in the receipts and payments account for **each** of the following.

(i) subscriptions

(ii) rent

(d) Explain the significance of the balance in the receipts and payments account:

(i) on 1 January 20-2

(ii) on 31 December 20-2

(e) Explain why the depreciation of the club's non-current assets does not appear in the receipts and payments account.

92. The Mahamba Sports Club had the following assets and liabilities on 1 April 20-5.

	$
Clubhouse at cost	57 000
Sports equipment at book value	15 000
Cash at bank	3 000
Subscriptions owing by members	200
Insurance prepaid	140

The following is a summary of the receipts and payments for the year ended 31 March 20-6.

Receipts	$	Payments	$
Subscriptions	5500	Insurance for 12 months	
Competition entrance fees	950	to 30 June 20-6	624
Proceeds of sale of old		Competition expenses	370
sports equipment	1000	Office expenses	183
Interest received	30	New sports equipment	2200
		Repairs and maintenance	97

The following additional information is available.

1 The old equipment disposed of during the year was sold at book value.

2 Sports equipment is depreciated by 10% on the book value of equipment held at the end of each financial year.

3 The club has 500 members who each pay an annual subscription of $100.

(a) Prepare the income and expenditure account of the Mahamba Sports Club for the year ended 31 March 20-6.

(b) Prepare the balance sheet of the Mahama Sports Club at 31 March 20-6.

74   *Cambridge O Level Principles of Accounts Workbook*

93. The following is the receipts and payments account of the Ansari Rugby Club for the year ended 31 May 20-6.

Receipts	$	Payments	$
Opening balance	769	Rent	2000
Subscriptions	4750	Rates	1950
Proceeds of sale of old		General expenses	486
equipment	198	New equipment	2000
Sales of refreshments	290	Repairs to equipment	282
Closing balance	918	Cost of refreshments	207
	6925		6925

The following additional information is available at 31 May 20-6.
1   Subscriptions prepaid amounted to $90.
2   Subscriptions accrued amounted to $170.
3   Rates prepaid amounted to $30.
4   General expenses accrued amounted to $93
5   The equipment sold had a book value of $250.
6   Equipment is to be depreciated by $380.

(a) Prepare an income and expenditure account of the Ansari Rugby Club for the year ended 31 May 20-6.

(b) Select **one** item appearing in the receipts and payments account which should not be included in the income and expenditure account and explain why it does not appear.

(c) Select **one** item appearing in the income and expenditure account which is not included in the receipts and payments account and explain why it does not appear.

(d) In connection with a club, explain what is meant by accumulated fund and how it arises.

94. The Scar Top Athletics Society was formed on 1 October 20-4. The treasurer provided the following information at the end of the first financial year.

		$
Receipts	Subscriptions	4820
	Shop sales	8100
	Competition ticket sales	1020
	Interest received	44
Payments	General expenses	585
	Purchase of shop fittings	1000
	Payments to credit suppliers for shop stock	3905
	Wages of shop assistant	3750
	Rent and rates	3190
	Insurance	1070
	Competition expenses	950

Structured Accounting Questions 75

At 30 September 20-5 –

1 Subscriptions prepaid amounted to $160.
2 $415 was owing to shop suppliers.
3 General expenses prepaid amounted to $15.
4 $284 rent was accrued.
5 The shop inventory was valued at $370.
6 Shop fittings are to be depreciated by $150.

(a) Prepare the income statement of the Scar Top Athletics Society Shop for the year ended 30 September 20-5.
(b) Prepare the income and expenditure account of the Scar Top Athletics Society for the year ended 30 September 20-5.

95. The treasurer of the Kaunda Street Music Society did not maintain a full set of accounting records but was able to provide the following information.

	1 December 20-1 $	30 November 20-2 $
Subscriptions owing by members	330	420
Subscriptions prepaid by members	–	150
Inventory of refreshments	466	514
Trade payables for refreshments	319	293

During the year ended 30 November 20-2 –

	$
Subscriptions received	4860
Payments to credit suppliers for refreshments	3861
Receipts from sale of refreshments	5982

(a) Prepare the subscriptions account for the year ended 30 November 20-2.
(b) Calculate the credit purchases for the year ended 30 November 20-2.
(c) Prepare the refreshments income statement of the Kaunda Street Music Society for the year ended 30 November 20-2.

*96. The financial year of the Island Drama Society ends on 31 July.
The treasurer has not maintained a full set of accounting records but was able to provide the following information.

At 1 August 20-3 –

	$
Premises at cost	33 000
Equipment at book value	17 500
Subscriptions prepaid by members	150
Subscriptions owed by members	320
Cash at bank	2 890
Staff wages accrued	350
Insurance prepaid	120

76 *Cambridge O Level Principles of Accounts Workbook*

During the year ended 31 July 20-4 –

Receipts	$	Payments	$
Subscriptions	5880	Insurance for 12 months	
Concert ticket sales	1943	to 30 September 20-4	744
Sale of old equipment (at		Concert expenses	1007
book value)	500	Wages	2290
		New equipment	2900

General expenses were paid during the year, but no record was made of the amount spent.

At 31 July 20-4 –
1   Subscriptions owed by members amounted to $90.
2   Wages accrued amounted to $290.
3   Equipment is being depreciated by 20% per annum on the book value of equipment held at the end of each financial year.
4   There was $3402 in the bank account.

(a)   Calculate the Island Drama Society's accumulated fund on 1 August 20-3.
(b)   Calculate the amount paid for general expenses during the year ended 31 July 20-4.
(c)   Prepare the Island Drama Society's income and expenditure account for the year ended 31 July 20-4.
(d)   Prepare the Island Drama Society's balance sheet at 31 July 20-4.

Chapter 18   Partnership Accounts – Part A

97. Precious and Marcia Minja are in partnership. Their partnership agreement includes the following.

> Interest on capital to be paid at 5% per annum
> Interest on drawings to be charged at 3% per annum
> Marcia Minja to receive an annual salary of $12 000
> Profits and losses to be shared 3:2

On 1 June 20-1 the balances on the partners' capital accounts were –

	$
Precious	90 000
Marcia	70 000

During the year ended 31 May 20-2 the partners' drawings were –

	$
Precious	15 000
Marcia	21 000

The profit for the year ended 31 May 20-2 was $25 100.
(a)   Prepare the profit and loss appropriation account of Precious and Marcia Minja for the year ended 31 May 20-2.

Structured Accounting Questions   77

(b) State why it is advisable for partners to draw up a partnership agreement when they form a partnership.

(c) State why a partnership agreement may provide for **each** of the following.
  (i) interest on capital
  (ii) interest on drawings
  (iii) partnership salaries

98. John and David Ngala are in partnership sharing profits and losses equally.

The following information is available for the year ended 31 January 20-8.

		$
Profit for the year		14 200
Interest on drawings –	John	220
	David	180
Interest on capital –	John	1 500
	David	1 200
Partners' salaries –	John	8 000
	David	6 000

(a) Calculate the profit/loss available for distribution. Show how this is divided between the partners.

On 1 February 20-7 the balances on the partners' current accounts were as follows:

	$
John	1 750 debit
David	2 260 credit

During the year ended 31 January 20-8 the partners' drawings were as follows:

	$
John	11 000
David	8 000

(b) Write up the current accounts of John and David Ngala for the year ended 31 January 20-8 as they would appear in the ledger of the partnership. Balance the accounts on 31 January 20-8 and bring down the balances on 1 February 20-8.

On 1 February 20-8 the balances on the partners' capital accounts were as follows:

	$
John	50 000
David	40 000

On 2 February 20-8 John transferred $3000 from the debit balance on his current account to his capital account. On 3 February David paid additional capital into the business bank account so that his capital was equal to that of John.

(c) Write up the capital accounts of John and David Ngala for the month of February 20-8 as they would appear in the ledger of the partnership. Balance the accounts and bring down the balances on 1 March 20-8.

78   *Cambridge O Level Principles of Accounts Workbook*

99. Terry and Candy Foo are in partnership. Their financial year ends on 31 August.

Their partnership agreement included the following.

Interest on capital to be allowed at 6% per annum
Interest on drawings to be charged at 4% per annum
Candy to receive an annual salary of $17 000
Profits and losses to be shared 2:1

The balances on the partners' accounts on 1 September 20-4 were as follows:

		$
Capital accounts –	Terry Foo	80 000
	Candy Foo	50 000
Current accounts –	Terry Foo	3 250 debit
	Candy Foo	1 050 credit

During the year ended 31 August 20-5, the partners' drawings were as follows:

	$
Terry Foo	12 000
Candy Foo	18 000

The income statement for the year ended 31 August 20-5 showed a profit for the year of $39 500.

(a) Prepare the profit and loss appropriation account of Terry and Candy Foo for the year ended 31 August 20-5.

(b) Write up the current accounts of Terry and Candy Foo for the year ended 31 August 20-5 as they would appear in the ledger of the partnership. Balance the accounts on 31 August 20-5 and bring down the balances on 1 September 20-5.

(c) Prepare a relevant extract from the balance sheet of Terry and Candy Foo at 31 August 20-5 to show their capital and current accounts.

100. Bill and Ben are in partnership. Their financial year ends on 31 March. Their share profits and losses in proportion to the capital invested.

On 1 April 20-3 the balances on the partners' capital and current accounts were –

	Capital account	Current account
	$	$
Bill	50 000	2 950 credit
Ben	25 000	1 700 debit

During the year ended 31 March 20-4 the partners' drawings were –

	$
Bill	6 000
Ben	12 000

Structured Accounting Questions 79

The following information was extracted from the profit and loss appropriation account for the year ended 31 March 20-4 –

	$	$
Profit for the year		15 150
Interest on drawings – Bill	180	
Ben	360	540
		15 690
Interest on capital – Bill	1 500	
Ben	750	
	2 250	
Salary – Ben	6 000	8 250
Profit available for distribution		7 440

At 31 March 20-4 the following information was available –

	$
Non-current assets at book value	87 100
Current assets	38 300
Current liabilities	40 000
Non-current liabilities	12 000

Prepare the balance sheet of Bill and Ben at 31 March 20-4. The capital and current account of each partner should be shown. The calculation of the current account balances may either be shown within the balance sheet or as separate ledger accounts.

*101. Ravi and Iqra own a garden maintenance business. Their financial year ends on 30 April.

The partnership agreement provides for –

      Loan interest at 6% per annum on loans from partners

      Interest on capital at 5% per annum

      Profits and losses to be shared equally

The trial balance of Ravi and Iqra at 30 April 20-3 was as follows:

	$	$
Capital account Ravi 1 May 20-2		70 000
Capital account Iqra 1 May 20-2		40 000
Current account Ravi 1 May 20-2		1 020
Current account Iqra 1 May 20-2	150	
Drawings Ravi	12 200	
Drawings Iqra	11 820	
Loan Ravi		20 000
Loan interest	600	
Premises at cost	70 000	
Equipment at cost	21 000	
Provision for depreciation of equipment		4 200
Motor vehicles at cost	32 000	
Provision for depreciation of motor vehicles		8 000
Income from customers		106 075

(Continued)

80 *Cambridge O Level Principles of Accounts Workbook*

Wages	57 870	
Repairs to equipment	2 720	
Motor vehicle expenses	3 030	
Insurance	3 450	
General expenses	2 765	
Printing and stationery	320	
Bad debts	220	
Provision for doubtful debts		360
Trade receivables	8 000	
Bank	23 280	
Cash	2 540	
Trade payables		2 310
	251 965	251 965

The following additional information is available.
1 At 30 April 20-3 wages, $1090, were accrued.
2 At 30 April 20-3 insurance, $360, was prepaid.
3 Equipment is being depreciated at 20% per annum using the straight line method.
4 Motor vehicles are being depreciated at 25% per annum using the reducing balance method.
5 The provision for doubtful debts is maintained at 5% of the trade receivables at the end of each financial year.
(a) Prepare the income statement of Ravi and Iqra for the year ended 30 April 20-3.
(b) Prepare the profit and loss appropriation account of Ravi and Iqra for the year ended 30 April 20-3.
(c) Prepare the balance sheet of Ravi and Iqra at 30 April 20-3.

102. Nicola and Lydia Dube are traders. Their financial year ends on 31 October. The following trial balance was drawn up on 31 October 20-8 after the calculation of the gross profit.

	$	$
Capital account Nicola 1 November 20-7		10 000
Capital account Lydia 1 November 20-7		10 000
Current account Nicola 1 November 20-7		118
Current account Lydia 1 November 20-7		236
Drawings Nicola	2 100	
Drawings Lydia	1 900	
Discount received		630
Discount allowed	940	
Wages	5 670	
Rent and rates	2 120	
Furniture and fittings at cost	10 500	
Provision for depreciation of furniture and fittings		2 100
Motor vehicles at cost	19 000	
Provision for depreciation of motor vehicles		6 840
Motor vehicle expenses	950	

(Continued)

Trade payables		3 459
Trade receivables	3 850	
Provision for doubtful debts		179
Bad debts	540	
Bank		1 029
Cash	50	
Loan (repayable 1 January 20-9)		4 000
Loan interest	200	
Commission received		1 090
General expenses	3 116	
Inventory 31 October 20-8	7 745	
Gross profit		19 000
	58 681	58 681

The following additional information is available.

1 At 31 October 20-8 motor vehicle expenses, $105, were outstanding and rates, $48, were prepaid.

2 The furniture and fittings are being depreciated at 10% per annum using the straight line method.

3 The motor vehicles are being depreciated at 20% per annum using the reducing balance method.

4 The provision for doubtful debts is maintained at 4% of the trade receivables at the end of each financial year.

5 The partnership agreement provides for interest on capital at 4% per annum and for profits and losses to be shared Nicola 3/5 and Lydia 2/5.

(a) Starting with the gross profit prepare the income statement of Nicola and Lydia Dube for the year ended 31 October 20-8.

(b) Prepare the profit and loss appropriation account of Nicola and Lydia Dube for the year ended 31 October 20-8.

(c) Prepare the balance sheet of Nicola and Lydia Dube at 31 October 20-8.

103. Yassin and Muneen are in partnership, sharing profits and losses 2:1. Their financial year ends on 30 November.

Despite having little accounting knowledge, Yassin decided to attempt a set of financial statements for the year ended 30 November 20-6. The balance sheet he prepared was as follows:

	$
Premises at cost	50 000
Machinery at cost	24 000
Furniture and equipment at cost	18 000
Inventory	23 200
Trade receivables	11 600
Bank overdraft	5 150
Drawings – Yassin	8 400
Muneen	6 600
	146 950

(Continued)

82 *Cambridge O Level Principles of Accounts Workbook*

Trade payables	13 520
Provision for depreciation of machinery	4 800
Provision for depreciation of furniture and equipment	3 600
Capital – Yassin	55 000
Muneen	40 000
Profit for the year	19 780
	136 700
Balance	10 250
	146 950

The following errors were then discovered.

1 No entry had been made for depreciation of furniture and equipment for the year. This asset should be depreciated by 10% per annum using the straight line method.

2 A provision for doubtful debts of $232 should have been created at 30 November 20-6.

3 No adjustment had been made for insurance, $60, prepaid at 30 November 20-6.

4 The inventory at 30 November 2006 included goods costing $1200 which were damaged and regarded as unsaleable.

5 Cash, $50, had been omitted from the balance sheet.

(a) Calculate the corrected profit for the year ended 30 November 20-6. Show the division of the profit between the partners.

(b) Prepare the corrected balance sheet of Yassin and Muneen at 30 November 20-6, using a suitable form of presentation.

Chapter 19   Partnership Accounts – Part B

104. (a) Explain **two** reasons why two sole traders may decide to amalgamate their businesses.

(b) Explain why a sole trader should value his goodwill before amalgamating with another sole trader.

Jamil and Saida are sole traders. They agreed to amalgamate their businesses on 1 June 20-6. On that date their assets and liabilities were as follows:

	Jamil	*Saida*
	$	*$*
Furniture and fixtures	15 000	10 000
Trade receivables	3 940	2 870
Trade payables	950	580
Office equipment	3 300	2 800
Other receivables		50
Other payables	40	
Motor vehicles	15 500	
Bank	(1 750)	2 860
Goodwill (Intangible assets)	9 000	6 000

Structured Accounting Questions 83

They agreed that all the assets and liabilities should be taken over by the new business at the above values.

(c) Prepare the opening journal entry in the books of the partnership. A narrative is required.

(d) Prepare the opening balance sheet of the partnership at 1 June 20-6.

*105. Kate and Beth each run an advertising agency. Their assets and liabilities on 31 May 20-5 were as follows.

	Kate $	Beth $
Premises at cost	90 000	
Trade receivables	20 000	10 000
Balance at bank		12 000
Bank overdraft	8 000	
Equipment at book value	35 000	40 000
Other receivables		2 000
Other payables	6 000	
Long term loan		10 000
Motor vehicle at book value	9 000	16 000

(a) **(i)** Calculate the capital of Kate on 31 May 20-5. Show your workings.

(ii) Calculate the capital of Beth on 31 May 20-5. Show your workings.

Kate and Beth decided to amalgamate their business on 1 June 20-5. They decided that goodwill would not be recorded in the accounting records.

(b) **(i)** Explain the meaning of the term "goodwill".

(ii) Name **one** accounting principle which supports the partners in their decision not to record goodwill in the accounting records.

Kate and Beth agreed the following.

1 Kate's premises were to be revalued at $110 000.

2 Beth would dispose of half of her equipment personally.

3 Kate and Beth would each create a provision for doubtful debts of 2 ½% of their trade receivables.

4 Beth would repay the long-term loan from personal funds.

(c) **(i)** Prepare the capital account of Kate before the formation of the new business.

(ii) Prepare the capital account of Beth before the formation of the new business.

(d) Prepare the opening balance sheet of the new business on 1 June 20-5.

84 *Cambridge O Level Principles of Accounts Workbook*

106. Kwok and Yoshi are sole traders. Their summarised balance sheets on 30 April 20-3 were as follows:

	Kwok $	Yoshi $
Premises	90 000	
Furniture and fittings	15 000	5 000
Motor vehicles		18 000
Inventory	6 200	4 300
Trade receivables	6 400	7 200
Bank	3 920	
	121 520	34 500
Capital	104 000	30 000
Non-current liability	10 000	
Trade payables	7 520	4 150
Bank overdraft		350
	121 520	34 500

Kwok and Yoshi decided to amalgamate their businesses on 1 May 20-3. They agreed the following.

1   Kwok's goodwill was valued at $30 000 and Yoshi's at $12 000.
2   Kwok's premises were revalued at $110 000.
3   Yoshi was to retain a motor vehicle valued at $8000 for personal use.
4   Yoshi was to write off debts of $200 as irrecoverable.
5   Each trader was to create a provision for doubtful debts of 2% of trade receivables.
6   Kwok's inventory was revalued at $5800 and Yoshi's at $3800.

(a) Prepare the capital account of each sole trader before the formation of the partnership.

(b) Prepare the opening balance sheet of the partnership on 1 May 20-3.

107. Didier and Kolo are sole traders. Their summarised balance sheets on 28 February 20-1 were as follows:

	Didier $	Kolo $		Didier $	Kolo $
Capital	80 700	91 600	Premises	60 000	40 000
Long term loan	20 000		Machinery	35 000	25 000
Trade payables	8 940	9 310	Equipment		14 500
Bank	2 180		Inventory	9 500	8 100
			Trade receivables	7 320	6 110
			Bank		7 200
	111 820	100 910		111 820	100 910

They agreed to amalgamate their businesses on 1 March 20-1. The following terms were agreed.

1   Premises owned by Kolo were not to be taken over by the new business.
2   Premises owned by Didier were to be revalued at $65 000.

Structured Accounting Questions   85

3   Didier's inventory was to be revalued at $8800 and Kolo's at $7500.
4   Didier was to repay the loan from private funds.
5   Didier's goodwill was to be valued at $25 000 and Kolo's at $20 000.

(a)   Prepare the capital account of each partner before the formation of the partnership.

(b)   Prepare the opening journal entry of the new business on 1 March 20-1. A narrative is required.

Chapter 20   Accounts of Manufacturing Business

108.   The Apollo Manufacturing Company provided the following information for the year ended 30 June 20-5.

	$
Inventory of raw material 1 July 20-4	23 500
Inventory of raw material 30 June 20-5	21 500
Work in progress 1 July 20-4	9 880
Work in progress 30 June 20-5	10 040
For the year ended 30 June 20-5	
Purchases of raw material	287 560
Direct factory wages	199 450
Direct expenses	8 740
Indirect factory expenses	186 330

(a)   Explain **each** of the following terms.
   (i) Work in progress
   (ii) Direct expenses
   (iii) Indirect factory expenses

(b)   Calculate the prime cost.

(c)   Calculate the cost of production.

109. (a)   Explain the purpose of a manufacturing account.
  (b)   Explain the difference between the following.
    (i) Prime cost and cost of production
    (ii) Direct labour and indirect labour
  (c)   The Vasant Vihar Manufacturing Company provided the following information.

	1 January 20-4	31 December 20-4
	$	$
Inventory – raw material	16 650	17 720
Work in progress	18 222	19 115
Factory operatives' wages outstanding	1 850	1 990
Factory insurance prepaid	760	800

86 *Cambridge O Level Principles of Accounts Workbook*

For the year ended 31 December 20-4:

	$
Purchases of raw material	210 500
Carriage on raw materials	3 120
Wages – factory operatives	197 280
factory supervisors	32 100
Factory rent and rates	15 500
Factory insurance	4 800
Factory general expenses	12 700

The factory machinery cost $56 000. The depreciation on factory machinery up to 31 December 20-3 totalled $20 160. The machinery is being depreciated using the reducing balance method at the rate of 20% per annum.

Prepare the manufacturing account of The Vasant Vihar Manufacturing Company for the year ended 31 December 20-4.

110. Homi Modi Manufacturers Ltd provided the following information for the year ended 31 March 20-9.

	$
At 1 April 20-8	
Inventory of finished goods	16 380
Inventory of raw material	7 850
Work in progress	6 120
For the year ended 31 March 20-9	
Revenue (Sales of finished goods)	400 500
Purchases of finished goods	22 540
Purchases of raw material	98 730
Carriage on raw material	2 030
Wages – factory direct	95 680
factory indirect	37 250
office	74 600
sales people	44 870
Insurance	10 500
Light and heat	13 300
General expenses	18 210
Depreciation – factory machinery	9 750
office equipment	3 150
At 31 March 20-9	
Inventory of finished goods	13 280
Inventory of raw material	8 170
Work in progress	7 470

The expenses are apportioned as follows:

    Insurance and general expenses – factory 2/3 and office 1/3

    Light and heat – factory 4/5 and office 1/5

Select the relevant figures and prepare the following accounts.

(a) The manufacturing account of Homi Modi Manufacturers Ltd for the year ended 31 March 20-9.

(b) The trading account section of the income statement of Homi Modi Manufacturers Ltd for the year ended 31 March 20-9.

111. Strand Road Manufacturing Ltd makes cooking sauces. Their financial year ends on 30 June. The following information is available.

	1 July 20-4 $	30 June 20-5 $
Inventory of raw material	2 160	2 870
Inventory of jars and labels	3 120	3 390
Inventory of finished goods	8 190	7 940
Work in progress	1 195	1 825

	For the year ended 30 June 20-5 $
Revenue (Sales of finished goods)	295 600
Purchases of raw material	26 830
Purchases of jars and labels	15 250
Carriage on raw material	1 980
Direct factory wages	32 560
Indirect factory wages	6 120
Factory light and power	9 440
Factory general expenses	4 910
Depreciation factory machinery	5 500

Prepare the manufacturing account and the trading account section of the income statement of Strand Road Manufacturing Ltd for the year ended 30 June 20-5.

Chapter 21 Departmental Accounts

112. Sajjad is a trader. His business is divided into two departments – Department A and Department B. He provided the following information for the year ended 31 May 20-4.

	Department A $	Department B $
Revenue (Sales)	350 000	205 000
Sales returns	1 900	–
Purchases	202 100	128 200
Inventory 1 June 20-3	16 950	9 160
Inventory 31 May 20-4	17 230	7 840
Carriage inwards	1 200	–

(a) Explain the purpose of departmental income statements.
(b) Prepare the departmental income statement (trading account section) of Sajjad for the year ended 31 May 20-4. Amounts for each department and the totals should be shown.

113. Top Clothes is a clothing retailer which has two departments – Department A which sells ladies' clothing and Department B which sells men's clothing. The financial year ends on 30 September.

88   *Cambridge O Level Principles of Accounts Workbook*

The following information is provided for the year ended 30 September 20-3.

	Department A $	Department B $
Revenue (Sales)	650 000	326 000
Sales returns	–	1 000
Purchases	475 200	194 750
Inventory 1 October 20-2	39 500	16 340
Inventory 30 September 20-3	36 740	17 160
Carriage inwards		1 350

Prepare the departmental income statement (trading account section) of Top Clothes for the year ended 30 September 20-3. Total columns are **not** required.

Chapter 22   Limited Company Accounts

114. Dwight Ltd was formed several years ago. It stated that its authorised capital would be as follows –

	$
Ordinary shares of $0.5 each	500 000
6% Preference shares of $1 each	200 000

Dwight Ltd provided the following information at 31 May 20-8 –

	$
Issued share capital Ordinary shares of $0.5 each	350 000
6% Preference shares of $1 each	150 000
General reserve	32 000
Retained profits (Profit and loss account balance)	8 900
5% Debentures	50 000

(a) Calculate the number of ordinary shares Dwight Ltd has issued.

(b) Suggest **one** reason why Dwight Ltd has not issued all the available ordinary shares.

(c) Calculate the total annual dividend (in $) payable on the preference shares.

(d) Calculate the total amount of interest (in $) payable on the debentures.

(e) Explain how the retained profits have arisen.

(f) Explain how the general reserve has arisen.

(g) Explain the difference between dividends proposed and dividends paid.

(h) Explain why debenture interest paid appears in the income statement of a limited company but ordinary share dividends paid appear in the profit and loss appropriation account.

115. The financial year of Leroy Ltd ends on 31 July. The following information is available for the year ended 31 July 20-3.

	$
Issued share capital	
Ordinary shares of $1 each	80 000
5% Preference shares of $1 each	50 000

The profit for the year ended 31 July 20-3 **before** preference share dividend was $20 000.

The retained profits (profit and loss account balance) on 1 August 20-2 amounted to $7500.

During the year ended 31 July 20-3 an interim dividend of 2 ½% was paid on the preference shares.

At 31 July 20-3:
1 Six months' preference share dividend was to be accrued
2 It was decided to transfer $8000 to general reserve
3 It was decided that an ordinary share dividend of 7% would be paid.

The directors decided not to apply the IAS rules regarding proposed ordinary share dividend.

(a) Calculate the profit for the year ended 31 July 20-3 after the preference share dividend.

(b) Prepare the profit and loss appropriation account of Leroy Ltd for the year ended 31 July 20-3.

116. Horton Ltd provided the following information.

	$
Issued share capital –	
6% Preference shares of $1 each	100 000
5% Preference shares of $1 each	60 000
Ordinary shares of $0.50 each	200 000
General reserve	21 000
4% Debentures	30 000

The retained profits (profit and loss account balance) on 1 July 20-3 amounted to $18 500.

During the year ended 30 June 20-4 an interim dividend of $0.01 per share was paid on the ordinary shares.

The profit for the year ended 30 June 20-4 was $41 000 **before** charging debenture interest and preference share dividend.

On 30 June 20-4 –
1 A full year's debenture interest was accrued
2 A full year's preference share dividend was accrued
3 It was decided to transfer $9000 to general reserve
4 It was decided to pay an ordinary share dividend of $0.02 per share
The directors decided not to apply the IAS rules regarding proposed ordinary share dividend

(a) Prepare a relevant extract from the income statement for Horton Ltd to show the final profit for the year ended 30 June 20-4.

(b) Prepare the profit and loss appropriation account for Horton Ltd for the year ended 30 June 20-4.

90   *Cambridge O Level Principles of Accounts Workbook*

(c) Prepare relevant balance sheet extracts for Horton Ltd at 30 June 20-4 to show –

(i) the capital and reserves

(ii) the non-current liabilities

117. The following balances remained on the books of Keyton Ltd after the preparation of the income statement for the year ended 30 June 20-6.

	$
Non-current assets at cost	237 000
Provision for depreciation of non-current assets	65 000
Ordinary shares of $1 each	150 000
6% Debentures	30 000
Trade receivables	38 000
Trade payables	43 000
Other receivables	4 210
Other payables	3 660
Provision for doubtful debts	950
Balance at bank	11 130
Inventory	42 000
General reserve	15 000
Interim ordinary share dividend	3 000
Retained earnings 1 July 20-5	9 620
Profit for the year ended 30 June 20-6	18 110

On 30 June 20-6 it was decided:

To transfer $5000 to the general reserve

To pay a final ordinary share dividend of 7 ½%

The directors of Keyton Ltd decided not to apply the IAS rules regarding proposed ordinary share dividend.

(a) Prepare the profit and loss appropriation account of Keyton Ltd for the year ended 30 June 20-6.

(b) Prepare an extract from the balance sheet of Keyton Ltd at 30 June 20-6 to show the capital and reserves.

(c) Calculate the net current assets of Keyton Ltd at 30 June 20-6. Show your workings.

118. The financial year of Haley and Co Ltd ends on 31 August. The following information is available.

Issued share capital	$
Preference shares of $1 each	60 000
Ordinary shares of $1 each	100 000

The profit for the year ended 31 August 20-3 was $18 200 **before** preference share dividend.

During the year ended 31 August 20-3 an interim dividend of $3000 was paid on the ordinary shares.

Structured Accounting Questions 91

At 31 August 20-3:

1 The preference share dividend, $3600, was to be accrued
2 It was decided to transfer $5000 to general reserve
3 It was decided to pay a final ordinary share dividend of $5000.
- **(a)** Calculate the total percentage rate of the ordinary share dividend for the year.
- **(b)** Calculate the percentage rate of the preference share dividend for the year.
- **(c)** State the percentage rate of preference share dividend which should be paid (provided the cash is available) for the year ending 31 August 20-4.
- **(d)** Explain why it is not possible to state the percentage rate of ordinary share dividend which will be paid (provided the cash is available) for the year ending 31 August 20-4.
- **(e)** Suggest **one** reason why it was decided to make a transfer to general reserve.
- **(f)** Explain the term "interim" in connection with the ordinary share dividend.
- **(g)** Calculate the profit retained in the year ended 31 August 20-3.

*119. The financial year of Napier Ltd ends on 31 May.

After the preparation of the income statement for the year ended 31 May 20-9 the following balances remained on the books.

	$	$
6% Preference shares of $1		50 000
Ordinary shares of $1		120 000
4% Debentures		50 000
General reserve		10 000
Retained profits 1 June 20-8		5 200
Inventory 31 May 20-9	25 320	
Trade receivables	21 400	
Trade payables		15 775
Provision for doubtful debts		428
Other receivables	833	
Other payables (debenture interest accrued)		2 000
Bank	31 300	
Premises at cost	129 000	
Machinery and equipment at cost	82 000	
Motor vehicles	28 000	
Provision for depreciation of machinery and equipment		32 800
Provision for depreciation of motor vehicles		15 750
Interim dividend on ordinary shares	3 600	
Profit for year before preference dividend		19 500
	321 453	321 453

92   *Cambridge O Level Principles of Accounts Workbook*

At 31 May 20-9 it was decided to:

Transfer of $4000 to general reserve

Pay the preference share dividend

Pay a final ordinary share dividend of 5%

The directors decided not to apply the IAS rules regarding proposed ordinary share dividend.

(a) Calculate the profit for the year after preference share dividend.

(b) Prepare the profit and loss appropriation of Napier Ltd for the year ended 31 May 20-9.

(c) Prepare extracts from the balance sheet of Napier Ltd at 31 May 20-9 to show
  (i) Non-current assets
  (ii) Net current assets
  (iii) Capital and reserves

Chapter 23   Analysis and Interpretation

120. Balbir is a trader. He provided the following information.

	$
At 1 March 20-4	
Inventory	9 800
For the year ended 28 February 20-5	
Revenue (Sales)	250 000
Purchases	190 300
Expenses	27 500
At 28 February 20-5	
Inventory	10 100
Total current assets	33 200
Total current liabilities	19 200
Total non-current assets	202 000

Calculate the following ratios to two decimal places.
(a) Gross profit to sales
(b) Net profit to sales
(c) Rate of inventory turnover
(d) Current ratio
(e) Quick ratio
(f) Return on capital employed (ROCE)

121. (a) Explain the meaning of **each** of the following terms.
  (i) Capital owned
  (ii) Capital employed

Structured Accounting Questions 93

(b) Usha is a trader. She provided the following information.

	$
For the year ended 30 June 20-5	
Cost of sales	120 900
Sundry expenses	14 100
Gross profit	35 100
Drawings	16 000
At 30 June 20-5	
Inventory	9 350

On 1 July 20-4 the inventory was $11 650 and Usha's capital was $150 000.

Calculate the following ratios (to two decimal places).

    (i) Gross profit as a percentage of sales
    (ii) Net profit as a percentage of sales
    (iii) Net profit as a percentage of Usha's capital on 30 June 20-5
    (iv) Rate of inventory turnover

(c)   **(i)** Explain the meaning of the term working capital.
    (ii) Explain **two** disadvantages of a shortage of working capital.
    (iii) State **two** ways in which the working capital of a business could be improved.
    (iv) State how **each** of the following transactions affect the working capital. Give a reason for your answer in each case.
      1 Purchase of goods, $500, on credit
      2 Purchase of non-current assets, $2500, by cheque
      3 Payment by cheque, $75, in full settlement of $80 owed to a creditor
      4 Sale of goods, $1000, on credit. The goods originally cost $800.

122. Ellis is a trader. He wishes to compare his position with that at the end of the previous financial year. He provided the following information.

At 31 August 20-7	$
Inventory	52 500
Trade receivables	38 000
Trade payables	41 400
Bank overdraft	5 200

(a) Calculate the following ratios. Calculations should be to two decimal places.
    (i) Current ratio
    (ii) Quick ratio

The following ratios were calculated on 31 August 20-6

Current ratio	2.00:1
Quick ratio	1.60:1

(b) Compare the ratios calculated in **(a)** with the above ratios.

94 *Cambridge O Level Principles of Accounts Workbook*

123. DEC Ltd provided the following information.

	31 May 20-4 $	31 May 20-5 $
Inventory	16 700	13 300

For the financial year ended 31 May 20-5 –

Revenue (Sales) – cash	105 000
credit	225 000
Purchases – credit	180 000

(a) Calculate the rate of inventory turnover correct to two decimal places.

(b) State **two** ways in which the rate of inventory turnover could be improved.

124. Emma is a trader. Her financial year ends on 31August. She provided the following information on 31 August 20-1.

	$
At 1 September 20-0	
Capital	180 000
10 year loan	20 000
For the year ended 31 August 20-1	
Gross profit	42 000
Cost of sales	210 000
Expenses	12 000

(a) **(i)** Calculate the percentage of gross profit to sales. The calculation should be correct to two decimal places.

(ii) State **two** reasons why this ratio is important to Emma.

(b) **(i)** Calculate the percentage of net profit to sales. The calculation should be correct to two decimal places.

(ii) State **two** reasons why this ratio is important to Emma

(c) **(i)** Calculate the return on capital employed (ROCE). Use the total capital employed on 1 September 20-0. The calculation should be correct to two decimal places.

(ii) State **two** reasons why this ratio is important to Emma.

(d) **(i)** Using the average inventory of $12 500, calculate the rate of inventory turnover for the year ended 31 August 20-0. The calculation should be correct to two decimal places.

(ii) State **two** ways in which Emma could improve the rate of inventory turnover.

Structured Accounting Questions 95

*125. Dave rented premises and started a business as a clothing wholesaler on 1 June 20-3. He sells on credit to large retail stores. Dave works full time in the business. He provided the following summarised financial statements.

Income Statement for the year ended 31 May 20-5

	$	$
Revenue (Sales)		230 000
Cost of sales		
Opening inventory	16 500	
Purchases	<u>175 100</u>	
	191 600	
Less Closing inventory	<u>14 500</u>	<u>177 100</u>
Gross profit		52 900
Expenses		<u>34 150</u>
Profit for the year		<u>18 750</u>

Balance Sheet at 31 May 20-5

	$	$
Non-current assets		195 000
Current assets	28 500	
Current liabilities	<u>13 500</u>	<u>15 000</u>
		210 000
Non-current liabilities		<u>50 000</u>
		<u>160 000</u>
Capital		<u>160 000</u>

(a) Calculate the following ratios correct to two decimal places.
- **(i)** Gross profit/sales
- **(ii)** Net profit/sales
- **(iii)** Rate of inventory turnover
- **(iv)** Return on capital employed
- **(v)** Return on capital owned (use the capital owned at 31 May 20-5)
- **(vi)** Current ratio
- **(vii)** Quick ratio

Dave's sisters, Ann and Susan, own a food retailing business. All goods are sold for cash.

The business was started ten years ago. Ann and Susan now own four shop premises. They do not work in the business any more but have appointed a manager for each of their four shops.

They provided the following information on 31 May 20-5.

Gross profit/sales	16.25%
Net profit/sales	14.75%
Rate of inventory turnover	24.30 times
Return on capital employed	15.20%
Return on capital owned	12.95%
Current ratio	3.25:1
Quick ratio	2.10:1

96   *Cambridge O Level Principles of Accounts Workbook*

(b) Compare the ratios calculated in **(a)** with those given above. Suggest reasons for the differences between the ratios.

(c) **Excluding** any factors mentioned above in connection with Dave, Ann and Susan, explain **five** problems of inter-firm comparison.

Chapter 24   Payroll Accounting

126. **(a)** Explain the purpose of a payslip.

(b) Explain the difference between a time sheet and a clock card.

Annie employs two part-time staff, Leena and Fatima. Leena is paid $5.50 per hour and Fatima is paid $6.20 per hour.

During the week ended 7 May 20-7, Leena worked for 44 hours and Fatima for 43 hours.

(c) Calculate the gross pay for each employee for the week ended 7 May 20-7. Show your workings.

127. Salim and Salman are employed in a factory and are paid $2.50 for each item they complete, subject to a minimum wage of $160 per week.

During the week ended 29 February 20-8, Salim completed 76 items and Salman completed 59 items.

(a) Calculate the gross wage for each employee for the week ended 29 February 20-8.

(b) Explain the difference between time basis and piece rate basis as methods of calculating wages.

128. Jasmine employs Nissar to manage her restaurant. Nissar is paid at the rate of $6 per hour for a normal working week of 38 hours. Any overtime is paid at the rate of time and a half, except for Sundays, when it is paid at double time.

During the week ended 31 July 20-1, Nissar worked the following hours.

Monday	4 hours
Tuesday	6 hours
Wednesday	7 hours
Thursday	7 hours
Friday	8 hours
Saturday	8 hours
Sunday	5 hours

(a) Calculate Nissar's gross pay for the week ended 31 July 20-1. Show your workings.

Weekly deductions from Nissar's gross pay are as follows:

Income tax at the rate of 20% on earnings over $200 per week

National insurance contributions at 10% of gross salary

Contribution of $10 to a private pension scheme

Contribution of $2 to a trade union

(b) Calculate Nissar's net pay for the week ended 31 July 20-1. Show your workings.

129. Ouyang provided the following information.

	For the week ended 30 June 20-5	Balance of account at 23 June 20-5
	$	$
Gross wages	2300	
Income tax	140	440
National insurance	220	655
Pension contributions	52	158
Trade union subscriptions	13	52

On 30 June 20-5 Ouyang paid his employees the net wages due in cash.

On the same date Ouyang sent cheques for the totals due in respect of statutory and voluntary deductions to the appropriate organisations.

Prepare journal entries (including those for cash and bank) to record the above transactions on 30 May 20-5. Narratives are required.

*130. Indira has four employees who are paid weekly in cash. They all pay the same rate of income tax and national insurance contributions and have the same voluntary deductions.

Indira pays all deductions from wages to the appropriate organisation at the end of each month.

For the week ended 14 January 20-1, all four employees worked for the same number of hours –

> 37 ½ hours at standard rate of $6 per hour
> 2 ½ hours at overtime rate of time and a half.

For the week ended 14 January 20-1 deductions from **each** employee's gross wages were made as follows:

Income tax	20% on earnings over $150
National insurance contributions	10% of gross pay
Contribution to pension plan	$5
Contribution to Wateraid charity	$1

(a) **(i)** Calculate the gross pay of **each** employee for the week ended 14 January 20-1 Show your workings.

(ii) State the total gross pay of the four employees.

(b) **(i)** Calculate the net pay of **each** employee for the week ended 14 January 20-1. Show your workings.

(ii) State the total net pay of the four employees.

(c) Calculate the total payable by Indira for the week ended 14 January 20-1 in respect of **each** of the following.

(i) Income tax

(ii) National insurance contributions

98 *Cambridge O Level Principles of Accounts Workbook*

    (iii) Pension plan contributions
    (iv) Wateraid charity contributions
  (d) Show the ledger entries (including cash and bank) Indira would make on 14 January 20-1.

Chapter 25 The Role of Information Technology and Professional Ethics

131. Curtis runs a mail order business, employing 35 people. He receives about 100 orders each week from customers who are asked to send a cheque on receipt of their orders. Curtis has 20 regular suppliers from whom he buys on credit terms.
Explain **four** uses to which ICT equipment could be applied to Curtis' financial records.

*132. Gurbir runs a small business and uses a manual system for her accounting records. She is considering installing a computer-based system.
  (a) Explain **three** advantages of such a system.
  (b) Explain **three** disadvantages of such a system.
  (c) State **three** costs which Gurbir would incur when installing and operating such a system.
  (d) State **three** accounting processes for which a computer system would be useful.

133. Ambrose was disappointed with the results shown by his draft financial statements. He thought that the profit could be improved and made the following suggestions to his accountant.

    Omit depreciation of machinery for this financial year
    Value the closing inventory at selling price

Explain why Ambrose's accountant would consider it professionally unethical to apply the above suggestions.

134. Janice has a small factory making beauty preparations and slimming aids. She pays her workers the minimum wage and applies the minimum statutory safety regulations when they are handling chemical substances. Measures have been taken to try to minimise the release of chemicals.

Janice has been offered the opportunity to purchase a range of slimming aids from another country at a very low price. She believes these could be sold at 400% mark-up. If Janice decides to purchase these products, she would reduce the scale of manufacturing and only retain the workers producing beauty products.

Discuss the ethical factors Janice should consider with regard to both the present situation and the possible future changes.

Appendix

Answers to Questions

Chapter 1

1. Bookkeeping is the detailed recording of all the financial transactions of a business. Accounting uses the bookkeeping records to prepare financial statements at regular intervals.
2. **(a)** Assets = Capital + Liabilities
   (b) **(i)** $35 000 **(ii)** $192 000 **(iii)** $23 000 **(iv)** $72 000
3. **(b)** asset **(c)** asset **(d)** liability **(e)** asset **(f)** asset **(g)** asset
4. **(b)** assets – machinery increase: liabilities – trade payables increase
   (c) assets – bank decrease: liabilities – trade payables decrease
   (d) assets – trade receivables increase: assets – cash decrease
   (e) assets – bank increase: liabilities – loans increase
5. Assets – premises $100 000, fixtures $31 000, inventory $19 500, trade receivables $12 500, bank $19 500: Liabilities – capital $168 000, trade payables $14 500

Chapter 2

7. **(a)** debit rent credit bank **(b)** debit purchases credit cash **(c)** debit carriage inwards credit cash **(d)** debit equipment credit WR Stores **(e)** debit Jones credit sales **(f)** debit sales returns credit Jones **(g)** debit drawings credit purchases
8. Cash account debit – balance $100, sales $840, balance b/d $718:
   credit – office expenses $22, drawings $200, balance c/d $718
   Bank account debit – balance b/d $2750, Wahid $280, AB Loans $5000, commission received $150, balance b/d $3350: credit – equipment $4500, Sabena $330, balance c/d $3350

100 *Cambridge O Level Principles of Accounts Workbook*

9. Bank account debit – capital $20 000, Aswan Traders $1000, balance b/d $17 500: credit – rent $500, Mohamed $3000, balance c/d $17 500.
Capital account credit – bank $20 000
Rent account debit – bank $500
Purchases account debit – Mohamed $3300
Mohamed account debit – purchases returns $100, bank $3000, balance c/d $200: credit – purchases $3300, balance b/d $200
Purchases returns account credit – Mohamed $100
Aswan Traders account debit – sales $1700, balance b/d $700: credit – bank $1000, balance c/d $700
Sales account credit – Aswan Traders $1700, cash $1500
Cash account debit – commission received $120, sales $1500, balance b/d $1100: credit – sundry expenses $20, drawings $500, balance c/d $1100
Commission received account credit – cash $120
Sundry expenses account debit – cash $20
Drawings account debit – cash $500

10. **(a)** Debit column – balance b/d $450, sales $1200, sales $590: credit column – sales returns $50, cash $250, bank $1000: balance column – $450 Dr, $1650 Dr, $1600 Dr, $1350 Dr, $1940 Dr, $940 Dr.
    (b) The balance of the account is shown after every transaction.

12. **(a)** Mar 1 Amount owed to Akinola by Anwar. Double entry – credit Anwar account for February
    Mar 9 Akinola sold goods on credit to Anwar. Double entry – credit sales account
    Mar 12 Anwar returned goods to Akinola. Double entry – debit sales returns account
    Mar 18 Anwar paid Akinola by cheque. Double entry – debit bank account
    Mar 31 Amount owed to Akinola by Anwar. Double entry – debit Anwar account for April
    (b) Mar 10 Akinola withdrew $100 from the business bank account for personal use.
    Double entry – credit bank account
    Mar 28 Akinola took goods from the business for personal use. Double entry – credit purchases account
    Mar 31 The total drawings for the month is transferred to Akinola's capital account. Double entry – debit capital account

Chapter 3

13. **(a)** **(i)** to check the arithmetical accuracy of the double entry bookkeeping
    (ii) to assist in the preparation of financial statements

Answers to Questions 101

(b) Any two from – error of commission, error of complete reversal, error of omission, error of original entry, error of principle, compensating errors. See the textbook for explanations.

(c) Error 1 is an error of original entry so will not affect the balancing of the trial balance.
Error 2 will affect the balancing of the trial balance as only one entry has been made rather than a double entry.
Error 3 is an error of omission when a transaction was completely omitted so will not affect the balancing of the trial balance.

14. Debit column – cash $600, equipment $18 200, fixtures and fittings $6100, trade receivables $12 400, purchases $48 600, sales returns $3300, wages $21 400, office expenses $4700, carriage inwards $900, sundry expenses $4000, drawings $12 500
Credit column – bank overdraft $10 500, trade payables $13 600, sales $66 200, capital $42 400
Trial balance totals $132 700

15. Debit column – premises $60 000, fixtures and fittings $13 500, inventory $9500, trade receivables $14 200, cash at bank $2300, purchases $36 100, sales returns $1400, rent and rates $4700, wages $12 300, general expenses $2500, carriage outwards $2600
Credit column – trade payables $9800, Loan from XY Finance $5000, sales $45 900, capital $98 400
Trial balance totals $159 100

Chapter 4

17. (a) More convenient to use **or** allows the maintaining of the ledger to be divided between several people

(b) **(ii)** nominal ledger **(iii)** nominal ledger **(iv)** sales ledger **(v)** purchases ledger **(vi)** nominal ledger

18. (a) Cash column debit – balance b/d $200, sales $950, balance b/d $210: credit – carriage outwards $40, bank $900, balance c/d $210
Bank column debit – balance b/d $4960, C Wright $1310, cash $900, balance c/d $2370: credit – Western Stores $2120, drawings $500, insurance $1420, motor vehicle $5500, balance b/d $2370

(b) An item appearing on both sides of the cash book. They occur when cash is paid into the business bank account and when cash is withdrawn from the bank for business use.

(c) It is not possible to take out more cash than is available so the cash balance can never be brought down as a credit balance. It can only be either a debit balance or a nil balance.

(d) The cash balance is an asset and the bank balance is a liability.

19. (a) Cash column debit – balance b/d $135, bank $1000, balance b/d $275: credit – wages $860, balance c/d $275
Bank column debit – High Street Stores $50, sales $1670, Valley Stores $192, balance c/d $3959: credit – balance b/d $3150, High Street Stores (dishonoured cheque) $50, Marine traders $936, Seafresh Foods $735, cash $1000, balance b/d $3959

102 *Cambridge O Level Principles of Accounts Workbook*

Discount allowed column – Valley Stores $8
Discount received column – Marine Traders $24, Seafresh Foods $15

(b) To encourage credit customers to pay their accounts promptly

(c) $24/(936 + 24) \times 100 = 2\,\frac{1}{2}\%$

(d) Credit Valley Stores account – discount allowed $8

(e) The total of the discount allowed account is transferred to the debit of the discount allowed account and the total of the discount received account is transferred to the credit of the discount received account.

20.(a)/(c) Cash column debit – bank $200, balance b/d $30: credit – motor expenses $150, carriage outwards $20, balance c/d $30
Bank column debit – capital $20 000, HiFinance Loan $6000, Honey Farm $1950, balance b/d $20 045: credit – cash $200, rent $350, motor vehicle $5900, BeeLine & Co $1455, balance c/d $20 045
Discount allowed column – Honey Farm $50
Discount received column – BeeLine & Co $45
Honey Farm account debit – sales $2100: credit – sales returns $100, bank $1950, discount $50
BeeLine & Co account debit – bank $1455, discount $45, balance c/d $930: credit – purchases $1500, purchases $930, balance b/d $930
Capital account credit – bank $20 000
Rent account debit – bank $350
Purchases account debit – BeeLine & Co $1500, BeeLine & Co $930
HiFinance Loan account credit – bank $6000
Motor vehicles account debit – bank $5900
Motor expenses account debit – cash $150
Sales account credit – Honey Farm $2100
Sales returns account debit – Honey Farm $100
Carriage inwards account debit – cash $20

(b) Discount allowed account debit – total for month $50
Discount received account credit – total for month $45

(d) Trial balance debit column – cash $30, bank $20 045, rent $350, purchases $2430, motor vehicles $5900, motor expenses $150, sales returns $100, carriage inwards $20, discount allowed $50
Trial balance credit column – BeeLine & Co $930, capital $20 000, HiFinance Loan $6000, sales $2100, discount received $45
Trial balance totals $29 075

Chapter 5

22. A statement of account is a summary of the transactions for the period and acts as a reminder to the customer of the amount due. It can be checked against the customer's own records to ensure that no errors have been made by either the supplier or the customer.

23. A debit note is issued by a customer. It is a means of notifying the supplier of any shortages, overcharges and faults and requesting a reduction in the total of the invoice. It is only when/if the supplier agrees and a credit note is issued that entries are made in the accounting records.

Answers to Questions 103

24. **(a)** invoice: Lydia **(b)** debit note: Tracey **(c)** credit note: Lydia **(d)** statement of account: Lydia **(e)** cheque: Tracey **(f)** receipt: Lydia

25. **(a)** Documents used – cheque, credit note, invoice
   (b) Debit note is not used as it is a request for the original invoice total to be reduced. No entries can be made until this request is accepted.
   Statement of account is not used as it is a summary of the transactions for the period and a reminder to the customer of the amount outstanding.

26. **(a)** Building Supplies
   (b) **(i)** $110 **(ii)** $50 **(iii)** $450 **(iv)** $90 **(v)** $360
   (c) **(vi)** discount
   (d) Trade discount may be allowed because the customer is in the same trade, and because the customer is buying in bulk.
   (e) $360 – 2 ½% = $351
   (f) **(i)** debit Peter Onamusi credit sales
   (ii) debit purchases credit Building Supplies

Chapter 6

28. Any five from – cash book, petty cash book, sales journal, purchases journal, sales returns journal, purchases returns journal, general journal.

29. Removes much detail from the ledger. Means that bookkeeping can be divided between several people.

30. The total of the purchases journal will be debited to the purchases account in the general ledger. The individual items will be credited to the accounts of the suppliers in the purchases ledger.

31. **(a)** Purchases journal – Pet Products Ltd $560, Cosy Canines $634, Pampered Pets & Co $422, Total $1616.
   Purchases returns journal – Cosy Canines $28, Pampered Pets & Co $12, Total $40
   (b) Purchases account debit – credit purchases for month $1616
   Purchases returns account credit – returns for month $40
   Pet Products Ltd account credit – purchases $560
   Cosy Canines account credit – purchases $634: debit – purchases returns $28
   Pampered Pets & Co account credit – purchases $422: debit – purchases returns $12
   (c) Purchases account and purchases returns account – general ledger
   Pet Products Ltd account, Cosy Canines account and Pampered Pets & Co account – purchases ledger

Chapter 7

33. **(a)** Gross profit is the profit earned on the goods sold. It is found by deducting the cost of sales from the sales. Net profit is the final profit after taking into account all running expenses and other income. It is found by adding other income to the gross profit and deducting the expenses.

104   *Cambridge O Level Principles of Accounts Workbook*

(b) The cost of sales = opening inventory + net purchases – closing inventory
The net purchases = purchases – purchases returns + carriage inwards – goods for own use

34. Total purchases – debit income statement: credit purchases account
Total sales returns – debit income statement credit sales returns account
Total general expenses – debit income statement credit general expenses account
Total rent received – debit rent received account credit income statement
Inventory 1 March 20-1 – debit income statement credit inventory account

36. Total income $86 300 (commission received $84 000, interest received $2300): less expenses $50 000 (rent and rates $12 000, general office expenses $8050, salary of assistant $25 000, postages and telephone expenses $4950): profit for the year $36 300

37. Revenue (sales) $78 000 (sales $80 000 less sales returns $2000): less cost of sales $36 500 (opening inventory $10 000, plus purchases $35 000, plus carriage inwards $7500, less closing inventory $16 000): gross profit $41 500 plus discount received $230 less expenses $47 450 (carriage outwards $5000, discount allowed $450, general expenses $18 000, wages $24 000): loss for the year $5720

Chapter 8

38. Machinery – non-current asset: inventory – current asset: trade payables – current liability: trade receivables – current asset: drawings – capital: cash – current asset: bank overdraft – current liability: 5 year bank loan – non-current liability: loss for the year – capital

39. (a) Non-current assets are usually arranged in increasing order of liquidity with the most permanent assets coming first e.g. premises, machinery fixtures, motor vehicles.

(b) Current assets are usually arranged in increasing order of liquidity, with the furthest away from cash coming first e.g. inventory, trade receivables, bank, cash.

(c) Net current assets is the difference between current assets and current liabilities.

40. Non-current assets – premises $80 000, fixtures and equipment $30 000, motor vehicle $15 000: current assets – inventory $12 000, trade receivables $9000, cash $200: current liabilities – trade payables $12 000, bank overdraft $4700: non-current liabilities – AB Loans $10 000: capital – opening balance $140 000, less loss for the year $11 500, less drawings $9000

41. Income statement – total income $146 000 (fees received $136 000, rent received $10 000): less expenses $96 400 (salaries $72 500, motor vehicle expenses $1480, discount allowed $2100, office expenses $13 570, rates and insurance $6750): profit for the year $49 600
Balance sheet – non-current assets – premises $50 000, office equipment $10 400, motor vehicle $9300: current assets – trade receivables $12 500, bank $13 900, cash $100: current liabilities – trade payables $1600: capital – opening balance $80 000, plus profit for the year $49 600, less drawings $35 000

Chapter 9

43. (a) The business is treated separately from the owner of the business. Only those transactions affecting the business are recorded in the accounting records of that business. For example, the purchase of motor vehicle by the business for business use would be recorded, but the purchase of a motor vehicle by the owner for personal use would not be recorded.

(b) The accounting records of a business are maintained on the basis of assumed continuity. It is assumed that the business will continue to operate for an indefinite period of time and that there is no intention to close down the business or reduce the size of the business significantly. For example, the non-current assets of a business will appear in the balance sheet at their book value: if it was intended to close the business these should be included at their expected sale values.

(c) Because reports of the progress of a business are required at regular intervals, the life of a business is divided into accounting periods. These are usually periods of 1 year. This allows meaningful comparisons to be made. For example, a set of financial statements is usually prepared at the end of each year which shows the profit earned during that period and the financial position at the end of the year; these statements can be compared with those for a previous financial period.

(d) All the assets and expenses of a business are recorded at their actual cost. This is a fact and can be easily verified. Inflation can make comparisons difficult when assets are purchased at different times. This principle is linked to the money measurement principle. For example, if premises are valued at $80 000 but the business managed to purchase them for $75 000 it is the latter figure which will be recorded in the accounting records.

44. Understandability

45. Information in accounting records can be useful if it can be compared with similar information about the same business for another accounting period or at another point in time. It is also useful to be able to make comparisons with similar information about another business. In order to make comparisons it is necessary to be aware of any different policies which may have been used and the effect of those policies on the accounting statements.

46. Any two from – free from significant errors, free from bias, prepared with suitable caution being applied to judgements and estimates, capable of being depended upon by users as being a true representation of the underlying transactions and events being represented.

47. (a) **(i)** capital expenditure **(ii)** revenue expenditure **(iii)** revenue receipt **(iv)** capital receipt

(b) Profit for the year will be overstated by $100

48. (a) **(i)** Capital expenditure is money spent on purchasing non-current assets, or improving and expanding existing non-current assets. These costs will appear in the balance sheet under non-current assets.

106 *Cambridge O Level Principles of Accounts Workbook*

       (ii) Revenue expenditure is money spent on running a business on a day-to-day basis. These costs will appear in the income statement where they are matched against the revenue for the period.

    (b) **(i)** capital expenditure **(ii)** capital expenditure **(iii)** revenue expenditure **(iv)** revenue expenditure **(v)** capital expenditure

50. Cost is the actual purchase price of the inventory, plus any additional costs incurred in bringing the inventory to its present position and condition. Net realisable value is the estimated receipts from the sale of the inventory, less any costs of completing the goods or costs of selling the goods.

51. **(a)** Inventory should be valued at the lower of cost or net realisable value.

    (b) Prudence

    (c) Profits and assets should not be over-stated and liabilities should not be under-stated so that the accounts present a realistic picture of the business. Profit is only recognised when it is realised.

Chapter 10

53. Wages account debit – total paid $68 000, balance c/d $1550: credit – balance b/d $1300, income statement $68 250, balance b/d $1550

Insurance account debit – balance b/d $1140, total paid $2400, balance b/d $1200: credit – income statement $2340, balance c/d $1200

54. **(a)** Rent received account debit – balance b/d $550, income statement $6600, balance c/d $1100: credit – total received $8250, balance b/d $1100

    (b) Income statement – other income – rent received $6600

    (c) Balance sheet – current liabilities – other payables (income prepaid) $110

56. Income statement – Revenue (sales) $350 000: less cost of sales $271 000 (opening inventory $20 000 plus purchases $280 000 less purchases returns $10 000, plus carriage inwards $5000 less closing inventory $24 000: gross profit $79 000 plus discount received $4100, plus rent received $6000 less expenses $69 390 (general expenses $12 200, rates and insurance $5090, repairs and maintenance $3870, salaries $44 500, motor vehicle expenses $2940, bank charges $790): profit for the year $19 710

Balance sheet – non-current assets – premises $80 000, fixtures and fittings $14 000, motor vehicle $9500: current assets – inventory $24 000, trade receivables $29 100, other receivables $900 (rent receivable due $500 prepayment $400): current liabilities – trade payables $23 300, other payables $3500, bank overdraft $17 990: capital – opening balance $110 000, plus profit for the year $19 710, less drawings $17 000

Chapter 11

58. **(a)** Depreciation is an estimate in the loss in value of a non-current asset over its expected working life.

    (b) Any two from – physical deterioration, economic reasons, passage of time, depletion.

Answers to Questions 107

(c) Depreciation is charged to avoid overstating the value of non-current assets as most lose value over a period of time. It also ensures that the cost of the non-current assets is spread over the years which benefit from the use of those assets. This also means that the profit is not overstated.

(d) Principles of prudence and matching

(e) (i) Straight line method of depreciation

$$\frac{\$20\ 000 - \$20\ 000}{5\ \text{years}} = \$3600 \text{ per annum}$$

(ii) Reducing balance method of depreciation

Year ended 31 July 20-2 – 40% × $20 000 $8000
Year ended 31 July 20-3 – 40% × ($20 000 – $8000) $4800
Year ended 31 July 20-4 – 40% × ($20 000 – $12 800) $2880

59. (a) Equipment account debit – Superquip $30 000, bank $10 000, balance b/d $40 000: credit – balance c/d $40 000
Provision for depreciation of equipment account debit – balance c/d $6000, balance c/d $13 000: credit – income statement $6000, balance b/d $6000, income statement $7000, balance b/d $13 000

(b) Income statement – expenses – depreciation of equipment $7000

(c) Balance sheet – non-current assets – equipment – cost $40 000, depreciation to date $13 000, book value $27 000

60. (a) (i) $9000 × 2 = $18 000: Machinery account debit – balance $18 000
(ii) 20% × $8 000 = $3600 × 3 years = $10 800: Provision for depreciation of machinery account credit – balance $10 800

(b) Machinery account debit – balance as described above, Western Ltd $12 000, balance b/d $21 000: credit – disposals $9000, balance c/d $21 000
Provision for depreciation of machinery account debit – disposals $5400, balance c/d $9600: credit – balance as described above, income statement $4200 ($1800 + $2400), balance b/d $9600
Disposal of machinery account debit – machinery $9000: credit – provision for depreciation $5400, cash $2800, income statement $800

62. (a) Income statement – total income $102 000 (fees received $102 000): less expenses $74 950 (general expenses $11 550, rates and insurance $10 080, wages $42 500, motor expenses $3650, loan interest $600, bank charges $140, depreciation fixtures and fittings $950, depreciation motor vehicles $4480): profit for the year $27 050

(b) Balance sheet – non-current assets – premises cost $55 000, fixtures and fittings book value $7600 (cost $9500, depreciation to date $1900), motor vehicles book value $17 920 (cost $28 000 depreciation to date $10 080): current assets – trade receivables $7800, other receivables $320: current liabilities – trade payables $590, bank overdraft $1300, other payables $300: non-current liabilities – loan QT Ltd $10 000: capital – opening balance $68 000, plus profit for the year $27 050, less drawings $18 600.

108   *Cambridge O Level Principles of Accounts Workbook*

Chapter 12

64. (a) Provision for doubtful debts account debit – balance c/d $165, balance c/d $186, income statement $39, balance c/d $147: credit – income statement $165, balance b/d $165, income statement $21, balance b/d $186, balance b/d $147

   (b) Balance sheet – current assets – 20-2 trade receivables $6200 less provision for doubtful debts $165, 20-3 trade receivables $6200 less provision for doubtful debts $186, 20-4 trade receivables $4900 less provision for doubtful debts $147

65. (a) J Mavuso account debit – balance b/d $480: credit – bank $450, bad debts $30

   (b) K Ngwenga account debit – balance b/d $1520: credit – bank $1064, bad debts $456

   (c) L Makamba account debit – balance b/d $250: credit – bad debts $250

   (d) Bad debts account debit – J Mavuso $30, K Ngwenga $456, L Makamba $250: credit – income statement $736

   (e) Provision for doubtful debts account – credit – income statement $800

66. Bad debts account

Oct 1 20-4 Amount owing by PK Stores was written off as a bad debt. Double entry – credit PK Stores account

May 1 20-5 Amount owing by Sellfast & Co was written off as a bad debt. Double entry – credit Sellfast & Co account

June 30 20-5 The total bad debts written off during the year was transferred to the income statement. Double entry – debit income statement

Provision for doubtful debts account

July 1 20-4 – The total provision at that date was brought down from the previous financial year. Double entry – debit provision for doubtful debts account for year ended 30 June 20-4

June 30 20-5 – This is the difference between the existing provision and that required at the end of the financial year ended on that date, and represents the surplus which is no longer required. Double entry– credit income statement

June 30 20-5 – This is the amount of the new provision for doubtful debts which is carried down to the start of the following financial year. Double entry – credit provision for doubtful debts account for the financial year commencing 1 July 20-5

68. Income statement – total income $44 420 (income from customers $42 000, commission received $2420): less expenses $36 856 (motor expenses $2788, insurance $1970, repairs and maintenance $2590, wages $26 100, bad debts $150, general expenses $353, provision for doubtful debts $15, depreciation equipment $740, depreciation motor vehicles $2150): profit for the year $7564

Balance sheet – non-current assets – equipment at valuation $10 120, motor vehicles at valuation $13 850: current assets – trade receivables $4085 (trade receivables $4300 less provision for doubtful debts $215) other receivables $62, bank $1040: current liabilities – trade payables $750, other payables $43: capital – opening balance $30 000, plus profit for the year $7564, less drawings $9200

Answers to Questions   109

69. **(a)** Income statement – total income $143 324 (gross profit $140 000, discount received $3200, reduction in provision for doubtful debts $124): less expenses $114 621 (rent $13 100, rates and insurance $8100, wages $79 500, office expenses $1978, general expenses $6380, bad debts $100, depreciation fixtures and fittings $3159, depreciation motor vehicles $2304): profit for the year $28 703

(b) Non-current assets – fixtures and fittings book value $28 431 (cost $39 000, depreciation to date $10 569) motor vehicles book value $9216 (cost $18 000, depreciation to date $8784): current assets – inventory $39 050, stationery inventory $122, trade receivables $23 474 (trade receivables $24 200 less provision for doubtful debts $726), bank $12 190: current liabilities – trade payables $31 500, other payables $80: capital – opening balance $70 000, plus profit for the year $28 703, less drawings $17 800

70. **(a)** Income statement – total income $44 984 (gross profit $42 000, commission receivable $2940, reduction in provision for doubtful debts $24) less expenses $40 784 (general expenses $4950, motor expenses $3260, bad debts $270, loan interest $600, wages $22 400 rates and insurance $3700, depreciation fixtures and equipment $3300, depreciation motor vehicles $2304): profit for the year $4200

(b) Balance sheet – non-current assets – premises at cost $60 000, fixtures and equipment book value $12 100 (cost $22 000 depreciation to date $9900), motor vehicles book value $9216 (cost $18 000 depreciation to date $8784): current assets – inventory $8200, trade receivables $9504 (trade receivables $9900 less provision for doubtful debts $396), other receivables $760 (prepayment $600, income receivable $160), bank $3200: current liabilities – trade payables $7480, other payables $300: non-current liabilities $10 000: capital – opening balance $86 500, plus profit for the year $4200, less drawings $5500

Chapter 13

71. Bank statement balance $3540 plus $1364 (cash sales $935, Hi-Fashion Ltd $242, Bermuda Road Boutique $187) less $781 (Beach Street Stores $295, Jamaica Road Boutique $182, Kingston Kids Ltd $304) Cash book balance $4123

72. **(a)** Cash book (bank columns) debit – balance b/d $3280, balance b/d $2321: credit – bank charges $109, insurance $850, balance c/d $2321

(b) Bank reconciliation statement – balance shown on bank statement $208, plus amounts not yet credited $1643 (cash sales), plus bank error $750, less cheques not yet presented $280 (Wilma), balance shown in cash book $2321

(c) Current asset $2321

73. **(a)** Cash book (bank columns) debit – balance b/d $8280, Aswan $2400, Ahmed $784, balance b/d $4669: credit – Ali $950, Hassan $3050, rates $685, wages $1550, rent $450, bank charges $110, balance c/d $4669

110 *Cambridge O Level Principles of Accounts Workbook*

(b) Bank reconciliation statement – balance shown on bank statement $5435, plus amounts not yet credited $784 (Ahmed), less cheques not yet presented $1550 (wages), balance shown in cash book $4669

(c) **(i)** Unpresented cheques are cheques that have been paid by the business and entered on the credit of the cash book but which do not appear on the bank statement.

(ii) Amounts not yet credited consist of cash and cheques that have been paid into the bank and entered on the debit side of the cash book, but which do not appear on the bank statement.

Chapter 14

75. (a) Debit – premises $85 000, fixtures and fittings $18 000, motor vehicle $11 500, inventory $9420, cash $200, bank $5100: credit – loan $20 000, capital $129 220

(b) Any three from – purchase of non-current assets, sale of non-current assets, non-regular transactions, correction of errors

(c) The journal is a book in which transactions are recorded before they are entered in the ledger. A journal entry is a note of what entries are required in the ledger with a short explanation of why these entries are required.

76. Debit sales $74 300, credit income statement $74 300: debit income statement $1040, credit rates $1040: debit income statement $4650, credit inventory $4650: debit equipment $5200, credit Superquip Ltd $5200: debit bad debts $56, credit Roddy $56: debit income statement $56, credit bad debts $56: debit inventory $5110, credit income statement $5110: debit income statement $790, credit provision for depreciation $790

77. (a) Debit income statement $33 100, credit purchases $33 100: debit income statement $1290, credit sales returns account $1290: debit discount received $870, credit income statement $870

(b) Debit drawings $100, credit general expenses $100: debit income statement $910, credit general expenses $910

(c) Debit disposal of motor vehicle $10 500, credit motor vehicles $10 500: debit provision for depreciation of motor vehicles $5124, credit disposal of motor vehicle $5124: debit Scrappers Ltd $4000, credit disposal of motor vehicle $4000: debit income statement $1376, credit disposal of motor vehicle $1376.

(d) Debit bad debts $140, credit Raj $140: debit income statement $411, credit bad debts $411: debit income statement $80, credit provision for doubtful debts $80

78. (a) Debit drawings $220, credit purchases $220: debit suspense $18, credit Kuso $18: debit motor vehicle expenses $199, credit motor vehicles $199: debit suspense $360, credit rent receivable $180, credit rent payable $180: debit office expenses $15, credit suspense $15: debit sales returns $100, credit suspense $100

(b) Suspense account debit – Kuso $18, rent receivable $180, rent payable $180: credit – difference on trial balance $263, office expenses $15, sales returns $100

(c) Only errors affecting the balance of a trial balance require a correcting entry in the suspense account. Errors 1 and 3 do not require entries in the suspense account as they do not affect the balancing of the trial balance.

80. (a) Statement of corrected profit for the year – profit for the year from income statement $1710: plus sales under-cast $500, prepayment $40, goods for own use $280: less depreciation of non-current assets $1750, bank charges $81, provision for doubtful debts $53, office expenses $20: corrected profit for the year $626

(b) Balance sheet – non-current assets book value $15 750 (cost $17 500 less depreciation to date $1750): current assets – inventory $1830, trade receivables $2597 (trade receivables $2650 less provision for doubtful debts $53), other receivables $40: current liabilities – trade payables $3100, bank overdraft $871: capital – opening balance $21 000, plus profit for the year $626, less drawings $5380

Chapter 15

81. (a) Purchases ledger control account debit – balance b/d $20, purchases returns $29, bank $1617, discounts received $33, sales ledger $90, balance c/d $1826: credit – balance b/d $1740, purchases $1860, interest $15, balance b/d $1826

(b) **(i)** cash book **(ii)** cash book **(iii)** journal

(c) When a business is both a supplier and a customer of the trader there will be an account in both the sales ledger and the purchases ledger. A contra item occurs when the balance on one account is set against the balance on the other account.

82. (a) Sales ledger control account debit – balance b/d $4520, sales $5180, interest $10 balance c/d $90, balance b/d $5387: credit – sales returns $210, bank $3977, discounts allowed $123, bad debt $58, purchases ledger $45, balance c/d $5387, balance b/d $90

(b) Any two from – to assist in locating errors, to prove the arithmetical accuracy of the sales ledger, to obtain the total owing by trade receivables quickly, to enable financial statements to be prepared quickly, to reduce fraud, to provide a summary of the transactions affecting debtors.

(c) Any two from – overpayment by a debtor, debtor returning goods after paying the account, debtor paying in advance for goods, cash discount not deducted before payment was made.

(d) $\dfrac{\$123}{(\$3977+123)} \times \dfrac{100}{1} = 3\%$

112   *Cambridge O Level Principles of Accounts Workbook*

83. (a) Purchases ledger control account debit – purchases returns $42, bank $2925, discounts received $75, sales ledger $212, balance c/d $4202, balance b/d $46: credit – balance b/d $3490, purchases $3920, balance c/d $46, balance b/d $4202

(b) Indicates an error either in the purchases ledger or in the purchases ledger control account.

(c) Any errors would not be revealed if the information in the purchases ledger was used as a source of information for the purchases ledger control account.

Chapter 16

85. (a) **(i)** Margin is the gross profit measured as a percentage of the selling price. **(ii)** Mark up is the gross profit measured as a percentage of the cost price.

(b) Revenue $40 000 (sales $40 200 less sales returns $200): less cost of sales $30 000(opening inventory $2300 plus purchases $31 600 less purchases returns $400 less closing inventory $3500: gross profit $10 000

86. Cost of sales $= 13.5 \times \dfrac{(\$3000 + \$4000)}{2} = \$47\ 250$

Purchases = $47 250 + $4000 – $3000 = $48 250
Income statement – Revenue (sales) $56 700: less cost of sales $47 250 (opening inventory $3000 plus purchases $48 250, less closing inventory $4000): gross profit $9450

87. (a) Statement of affairs – non-current assets – premises cost $80 000, fixtures and equipment cost $6000, motor vehicle cost $11 800: current assets – trade receivables $4100, bank $2500: current liabilities – other payables $600: non-current liabilities – loan – HiFinance Ltd $20 000: capital – balance $83 800

(b) Statement of affairs – non-current assets – premises cost $80 000, fixtures and equipment book value $5600 (cost $7000 less depreciation for the year $1400), motor vehicle book value $9440 (cost $11 800 less depreciation for the year $2360): current assets – trade receivables $4750: current liabilities – other payables $570, bank $1420: non-current liabilities – loan – HiFinance Ltd $10 000: capital – balance $87 800

(c) Calculation of profit for the year – increase in capital $4000 (capital at 31 August 20-6 $87 800 less capital at 1 September 20-5 $83 800): add drawings $4500: profit for the year $8500

89. (a) Total trade receivables account debit – balance b/d $4970, sales $44 280, balance b/d $5250: credit – bank $43 120, discounts allowed $880, balance c/d $5250

(b) Total trade payables account debit – bank $43 290, discounts received $1110, balance c/d $6950: credit balance b/d $6250, purchases $45 100, balance b/d $6950

Answers to Questions   113

(c)   Income statement – Revenue (sales) $60 000 (cash sales $15 720, credit sales $44 280): less cost of sales $46 200 (opening inventory $3870, purchases $45 430 (cash purchases $3100, credit purchases $45 100) less closing inventory $3100): gross profit $13 800

(d)   Rate of inventory turnover $= \dfrac{\$46\,200}{\$3870 + \$3100 \div 2} = 13.26$ times

90. (a)   Bank account debit – capital $16 000, debtors $68 386, balance b/d $8854: credit – creditors $57 915, general expenses $160, machinery repairs $120, wages $6556, rates and insurance $930, drawings $9850, balance c/d $8854

(b)   Total trade payables account debit – bank $57 915, returns $150, discounts received $1485, balance c/d $17 650: credit – purchases $77 200, balance b/d $17 650

(c)   Total trade receivables account debit – sales $83 000, balance b/d $11 300: credit – bank $68 385, sales returns $970, discounts allowed $2115, bad debt $230, balance c/d $11 300

(d)   Income statement – Revenue (sales) $82 030 (sales $83 000 less sales returns $970): less cost of sales $65 624 (purchases $77 200 less purchases returns $150, less goods for own use $1550, less closing inventory $9876): gross profit $16 406

(e)   Income statement – total income $17 891 (gross profit $16 406, discounts received $1485): less expenses $11 511 (general expenses $160, machinery repairs $120, wages $6556, rates and insurance $930, bad debts $230, discounts allowed $2115, depreciation machinery $1400): profit for the year $6380

(f)   Balance sheet – non-current assets – premises cost $50 000, machinery book value $12 600 (cost $14 000 depreciation to date $1400): current assets – inventory $9876, trade receivables $11 300, bank $8854: current liabilities – trade payables $17 650: capital – opening balance $80 000, plus profit for the year $6380, less drawings $11 400 (bank $9850, goods $1550)

Chapter 17

91. (a)   Receipts and payments account debit – balance b/d $420, subscriptions $1900, balance c/d $440: credit – clubhouse rent $824, insurance $320, general expenses $515, new furniture $1100

(b)   Any two from – R & P records all money received and paid (both capital and revenue items) but I & E records only revenue receipts and revenue expenditure: R & P does not have adjustments for accruals and prepayments but I & E does: R & P does not include non-monetary items, but I & E does.

(c)   **(i)** The total amount received ($1900) is included as this is the total money received during the year. No adjustment is required for accruals and prepayments.

114 *Cambridge O Level Principles of Accounts Workbook*

        (ii) The total amount paid ($825) is included as this is the total money paid during the year. No adjustment is required for the prepayment.

(d)   **(i)** The opening balance represents the money that the club possesses.

     (ii) The closing balance represents a bank overdraft (the amount the club owes the bank)

(e) Depreciation is not included as this is a non-monetary expense.

92. (a) Income and expenditure account – income $5610 (subscriptions $5000, profit on competition $580, interest received $30): less expenditure $2508 (insurance $608, office expenses $183, repairs and maintenance $97, depreciation sports equipment $1620): surplus for year $3102

(b) Balance sheet – non-current assets – clubhouse at cost $57 000, sports equipment at book value $14 580 ($15 000 – $1000 + $2200 – $1620): current assets – other receivables $156, bank $7006 ($3000 + $7480 – $3474): current liabilities – subscriptions prepaid $300: accumulated fund – opening balance $75 340, plus surplus for year $3102

93. (a) Income and expenditure account – income $4913 (subscriptions $4830, profit on refreshments $83): less expenditure $5213 (rent $2000, rates $1920, general expenses $579, repairs to equipment $282, loss on equipment $52, depreciation on equipment $380): deficit for year $300

(b) Any one from –

Opening balance – this represents the money owned by the club at the start of the year

Closing balance – this represents the money owed by the club to the bank at the end of the year (bank overdraft)

New equipment – this is capital expenditure and only revenue expenditure is included in the income and expenditure account

Proceeds of sale – this is a capital receipt. Only the loss or profit on the sale of as asset is included in the income and expenditure account

(c) Any one from –

Depreciation of equipment – this is a non-monetary expense and cannot, therefore, appear in the receipts and payments account

Loss on sale of equipment – this does not represent money received or paid and cannot, therefore, appear in the receipts and payments account

(d) Accumulated fund is the equivalent of capital in a business. It represents the accumulated surpluses made by the club (less any deficits).

94. (a) Income statement – Revenue (sales) $8100: less cost of sales $7850 (purchases $4320, less closing inventory $370, wages of shop assistant $3750, depreciation shop fittings $150): profit $250

(b) Income and expenditure account – income $5024 (subscriptions $4660, profit on shop $250, profit on competition $70, interest received $44) less expenditure $5114 (general expenses $570, rent and rates $3474, insurance $1070): deficit for year $90

95. (a) Subscriptions account – debit – balance b/d $330, balance c/d $150, income and expenditure $4800, balance b/d $420: credit – bank $4860, balance c/d $420, balance b/d $150

Answers to Questions 115

(b) Total trade payables account – debit – bank $3861, balance c/d $293: credit – balance b/d $319, purchases $3835, balance b/d $293

(c) Refreshments income statement – Revenue (sales) $5982: less cost of sales $3787 opening inventory $466, purchases $3835, less closing inventory $514: profit $2195

Chapter 18

97. (a) Appropriation account – Profit for the year $25 100, plus interest on drawings P $450, M $630: less appropriations $20 000 (interest on capital P $4500, M $3500; partner's salary M $12 000): share of profit P $3708, M $2472

(b) To avoid future disagreements and misunderstandings.

(c) **(i)** To compensate the partner investing the most capital

(ii) To deter partners from making drawings and to penalise the partner making the most drawings

(iii) To reward the partner who has the greatest share of the work and responsibilities

98. (a) Loss available for distribution – $2100 (Profit for the year $14 200 plus interest on drawings $400, less interest on capital $2700, less partners' salaries $14 000) Division of loss – $1050 each

(b) John Ngala current account – debit – balance b/d $1750, drawings $11 000, interest on drawings $220, share of loss $1050, balance b/d $4520: credit – interest on capital $1500, partner's salary $8000, balance c/d $4520
David Ngala current account – debit – drawings $8000, interest on drawings $180, share of loss $1050, balance c/d $230: credit – balance b/d $2260, interest on capital $1200, partner's salary $6000, balance b/d $230

(c) John Ngala capital account – debit – current account $3000, balance c/d $47 000: credit – balance b/d $50 000, balance b/d $47 000
David Ngala capital account – debit – balance c/d $47 000: credit – balance b/d $40 000, bank $7000, balance b/d $47 000

99. (a) Profit and loss appropriation account – Profit for the year $39 500, plus interest on drawings T $480, C $720: less appropriations $24 800 (interest on capital T $4800, C $3000, partner's salary C $17 000): share of profit T $10 600, C $5300

(b) Terry Foo current account – debit – balance b/d $3250, drawings $12 000, interest on drawings $480, balance b/d $330: credit – interest on capital $4800, share of profit $10 600, balance c/d $330
Candy Foo current account – debit – drawings $18 000, interest on drawings $720, balance c/d $7630: credit – balance b/d $1050, interest on capital $3000, partner's salary $17 000, share of profit $5300, balance b/d $7630

(c) Balance sheet – capital accounts – Terry Foo $80 000, Candy Foo $50 000, total $130 000: current accounts – Terry Foo ($330), Candy Foo $7630, total $7300: totals Terry Foo $79 670, Candy Foo $57 630, total $137 300

116 *Cambridge O Level Principles of Accounts Workbook*

100. Balance sheet – non-current assets at book value $87 100: current assets $38 300: current liabilities $40 000: non-current liabilities $12 000: capital accounts Bill $50 000, Ben $25 000: current accounts Bill $3230 (balance $2950, interest on capital $1500, profit share $4960, less drawings $6000, less interest on drawings $180) Ben ($4830) (balance ($1700), interest on capital $750, salary $6000, profit share $2480 less drawings $12 000, less interest on drawings $360)

102. (a) Income statement – total income $20 745 (gross profit $19 000, discount received $630, commission received $1090, reduction in provision for doubtful debts $25) less expenses $17 075 (discount allowed $940, wages $5670, rent and rates $2072, motor vehicle expenses $1055, bad debts $540, loan interest $200, general expenses $3116, depreciation furniture and fittings $1050, depreciation motor vehicles $2432: profit for the year $3670

(b) Profit and loss appropriation account – Profit for the year $3670, less appropriations $800 (interest on capital N $400, L $400): share of profit N $1722, L $1148

(c) Balance sheet – non-current assets – furniture and fittings book value $7350 (cost $10 500 depreciation to date $3150), motor vehicles book value $9728 (cost $19 000 depreciation to date $9272): current assets – inventory $7745, trade receivables $3696 (trade receivables $3850 provision for doubtful debts $154), other receivables $48, cash $50: current liabilities – trade payables $3459, other payables $105, other payables (short-term loan) $4000, bank overdraft $1029: capital accounts N $10 000, L $10 000: current accounts – N $140 (balance $118, interest on capital $400, profit share $1722, less drawings $2100) L ($116) (balance $236, interest on capital $400, profit share $1148, less drawings $1900)

103. (a) Statement of corrected profit – profit for the year from balance sheet $19 780: plus insurance prepaid $60: less depreciation of furniture and equipment $1800, provision for doubtful debts $232, damaged inventory $1200: corrected profit for the year $16 608 Division of profit – Y $11 072, M $5536

(b) Balance sheet – non-current assets – premises cost $50 000, machinery book value $19 200 (cost $24 000 depreciation to date $4800), furniture and equipment book value $12 600 (cost $18 000 depreciation to date $5400): current assets – inventory $22 000, trade receivables $11 368 (trade receivables $11 600 provision for doubtful debts $232), other receivables $60, cash $50: current liabilities – trade payables $13 520, bank overdraft $5150: capital accounts Y $55 000, M $40 000: current accounts Y $2672 (profit share $11 072 less drawings $8400), M ($1064) (profit share $5536 less drawings $6600)

Chapter 19

104. (a) Additional capital and additional skills

(b) The new business will benefit from the value of the goodwill built up by the sole trader, so goodwill should be included in the value he is contributing to the new business.

Answers to Questions 117

(c) Debit – goodwill $15 000, furniture and fixtures $25 000, office equipment $6100, motor vehicles $15 500, trade receivables $6810, other receivables $50, bank $1110: credit – trade payables $1530, other payables $40, capital J $44 000, capital S $24 000

(d) Balance sheet – non-current assets – intangible – goodwill $15 000, tangible – furniture and fixtures $25 000, office equipment $6100, motor vehicles $15 500: current assets – trade receivables $6810, other receivables $50, bank $1110: current liabilities – trade payables $1530, other payables $40: capital accounts J $44 000, S $24 000

106. (a) Capital account Kwok – debit – provision for doubtful debts $128, inventory $400, balance c/d $153 472: credit – balance b/d $104 000, goodwill $30 000, premises $20 000, balance b/d $153 472

Capital account Yoshi – debit – motor vehicle $8000, trade receivables $200, provision for doubtful debts $140, inventory $500, balance c/d $33 160: credit – balance b/d $30 000, goodwill $12 000, balance b/d $33 160

(b) Balance sheet – non-current assets – intangible – goodwill $42 000, tangible – premises $110, 000, furniture and fittings $20 000, motor vehicles $10 000: current assets – inventory $9600, trade receivables $13 132 (trade receivables $13 400 provision for doubtful debts $268), bank $3570: current liabilities – trade payables $11 670: non-current liabilities– loan $10 000: capital accounts K $153 472, Y $33 160

107. (a) Capital account Didier – debit – inventory $700, balance c/d $130 000: credit – balance b/d $80 700, premises $5000, loan $20 000, goodwill $25 000, balance b/d $130 000 Capital account Kolo – debit – premises $40 000, inventory $600, balance c/d $71 000: credit – balance b/d $91 600, goodwill $20 000, balance b/d $71 000

(b) Debit – goodwill $45 000, premises $65 000, machinery $60 000, equipment $14 500, inventory $16 300, trade receivables $13 430, bank $5020: credit – trade payables $18 250, capital D $130 000, capital K $71 000

Chapter 20

108. (a) (i) Work in progress is the goods which are partly completed at the end of the financial year.

(ii) Direct expenses are those expenses which a manufacturer can directly link with the product being manufactured.

(iii) Indirect factory expenses are sometimes referred to as factory overheads. These are costs of operating the factory which cannot be directly linked with the product being manufactured.

(b) Prime cost – $497 750 = Cost of material consumed $289 560 (Opening inventory raw materials $23 500, purchases of raw material $287 560, less closing inventory of raw material $21 500), direct factory wages $199 450, direct expenses $8740

(c) Cost of production – $683 920 = Prime cost $497 750, indirect factory expenses $186 330, opening work in progress $9880, less closing work in progress $10 040

118   *Cambridge O Level Principles of Accounts Workbook*

109. (a) The purpose of a manufacturing account is to calculate how much it has cost the business to manufacture the goods produced in the financial year.

(b) **(i)** Prime cost is the total of the three elements of cost – direct material, direct labour and direct expenses: cost of production is the prime cost plus the factory overheads.

(ii) Direct labour is the cost of the wages of the people who are employed in the factory making the goods: indirect labour is the cost of the wages of the people who are employed in the factory but who are not actually involved in the production of the finished goods.

(c) Manufacturing account – Cost of material consumed $212 550 (opening inventory raw material $16 650, purchases of raw material $210 500, carriage on raw material $3120, less closing inventory raw material $17 720), direct wages $197 420, prime cost $409 970, factory overheads $72 228 (wages factory supervisors $32 100, factory rent and rates $15 500, factory insurance $4760, factory general expenses $12 700, depreciation factory machinery $7168), opening work in progress $18 222, less closing work in progress $19 115, production cost of goods completed $481 305

110. (a) Manufacturing account – Cost of material consumed $100 440 (opening inventory raw material $7850, purchases of raw material $98 730, carriage on raw material $2030, less closing inventory raw material $8170), direct wages $95 680, prime cost $196 120, factory overheads $76 780 (factory indirect wages $37 250, factory insurance $7000, factory light and heat $10 640, factory general expenses $12 140, depreciation factory machinery $9750), opening work in progress $6120, less closing work in progress $7470, production cost of goods completed $271 550

(b) Income statement – revenue (sales) $400 500: less cost of sales $297 190 (opening inventory finished goods $16 380, production cost of goods completed $271 550, purchases finished goods $22 540, less closing inventory finished goods $13 280): gross profit $103 310

Chapter 21

112. (a) Departmental accounts show the profit or loss of each department separately, which are not revealed by an overall set of accounts. They also ensure that attention is drawn to a department which is not earning a profit, allowing improvements to be made as necessary.

(b) Income statement Department A – revenue (sales) $348 100 (sales $350 000 less sales returns $1900): less cost of sales $203 020 (opening inventory $16 950, purchases $202 100, carriage inwards $1200, less closing inventory $17 230): gross profit $145 080

Income statement Department B – revenue (sales) $205 000: less cost of sales $129 520 (opening inventory $9160, purchases $128 200, less closing inventory $7840): gross profit $75 480

Answers to Questions 119

Income statement Total – Revenue (sales) $553 100 (sales $555 000 less sales returns $1900): less cost of sales $332 540 (opening inventory $26 110, purchases $330 300, carriage inwards $1200, less closing inventory $25 070): gross profit $220 560

Chapter 22

114. (a) 700 000
   (b) So that further shares can be issued in the future when additional funds are required.
   (c) $9000
   (d) $2500
   (e) The retained profit is the total unappropriated profits which have not been distributed as dividends but have been retained within the company
   (f) The general reserve is the total of profits which have been transferred from the profit and loss appropriation account as a means of ploughing back profits within the company.
   (g) Dividends proposed are those dividends which remain unpaid at the end of the financial year. Dividends paid are sometimes referred to as interim dividends and are those dividends which have been paid to shareholders during the financial year.
   (h) Debenture interest paid appears in the income statement because it is interest on a loan. It is not an appropriation of profits as debenture holders are lenders not members of the company. Ordinary share dividend paid appears in the profit and loss appropriation account because it represents the share of the profit paid to the ordinary shareholders.

115. (a) Profit for the year $20 000 less preference dividend $2500 (paid $1250 + accrued $1250): profit for the year after preference share dividend $17 500
   (b) Profit and loss appropriation account – Profit for the year $17 500 less appropriations $13 600 (transfer to general reserve $8000, ordinary dividend $5600): retained profit for the year $3900, retained profit b/f $7500, retained profit c/f $11 400

116. (a) Extract from income statement – profit for the year before debenture interest and preference dividend $41 000, less debenture interest $1200, less preference dividend ($6000 + $3000): profit for the year $30 800
   (b) Profit and loss appropriation account – Profit for the year $30 800 less appropriations $21 000 (transfer to general reserve $9000, ordinary dividend paid $4000, ordinary dividend proposed $8000): retained profit for the year $9800, retained profit b/f $18 500, retained profit c/f $28 300
   (c) Balance sheet extracts –
       (i) Capital and reserves – 6% preference shares of $1 each $100 000, 5% preference shares of $1 each $60 000, ordinary shares of $0.50 each $200 000, general reserve $30 000, retained profit $28 300
       (ii) Non-current liabilities – 4% debentures $30 000

120 *Cambridge O Level Principles of Accounts Workbook*

117. (a) Profit and loss appropriation account – Profit for the year $18 110 less appropriations $19 250 (transfer to general reserve $5000, ordinary dividend paid $3000, ordinary dividend proposed $11 250): retained profit for the year ($1140), retained profit b/f $9620, retained profit c/f $8480
(b) Balance sheet extract – capital and reserves – ordinary share capital $150 000, general reserve $20 000, retained earnings $8480.
(c) Net current assets - $36 480: current assets $94 390(inventory $42 000, trade receivables $37 050 (trade receivables $38 000 less provision for doubtful debts $950), other receivables $4210, bank $11 130) less current liabilities $57 910 (trade payables $43 000, other payables $14 910 (other payables $3660, proposed dividends $11 250))
118. (a) 8% **(b)** 6% **(c)** 6%
(d) Ordinary share dividend is not a fixed annual amount (although many companies try to maintain a similar rate each year) but is dependent on the trading results of the company.
(e) A transfer to general reserve may be made to plough back a certain amount of profit to indicate that it is for long-term use within the company.
(f) The term interim refers to a "half-way" dividend which is paid during the financial year to which it relates.
(g) Profit for the year after preference dividend $14 600 ($18 200 – preference dividend $3600): less appropriations $13 000 (transfer to general reserve $5000, ordinary dividend (paid $3000, proposed $5000): profit retained in the year $1600

Chapter 23

120. (a) 24% **(b)** 13% **(c)** 19.10 times **(d)** 1.73:1 **(e)** 1.20:1 **(f)** 15.05%
121. (a) **(i)** Capital owned is the amount owed by a business to the owner(s) of that business.
(ii) Capital employed is the total funds which are being used by a business (owner's capital plus long term liabilities).
(b) **(i)** 22.50% **(ii)** 13.46% **(iii)** 13.55% **(iv)** 11.51 times
(c) **(i)** Working capital is the difference between the current assets and the current liabilities and is the amount available for the day-to-day running of the business.
(ii) Any two from – cannot meet liabilities when they are due: experience difficulties in obtaining supplies on credit: cannot take advantage of cash discounts; cannot take advantage of business opportunities when they arise.
(iii) Any two from – introduction of further capital by the owner(s): obtaining long term loans: selling surplus non-current assets: reducing drawings/dividends.
(iv) 1 No effect: current assets increase by $500 and current liabilities increase by $500.
2 Decrease $2500: current assets decrease by $2500 and non-current assets increase by $2500.

Answers to Questions   121

        3 Increase $5: current assets decrease by $75 and current liabilities decrease by $80.

        4 Increase $200: current assets increase by $200 (inventory decreases by $800 and debtors increase by $1000).

122. (a)   **(i)** 1.94:1 **(ii)** 0.82:1

    (b)   Current ratio slightly less in 20-7, but no significant changes: the current assets are almost double the current liabilities. The quick ratio has fallen by almost half: the liquid assets are now less than the current liabilities and the company may have problems paying debts when they fall due.

123. (a) 12.23 times

    (b) Reduce inventory levels and generate more sales activity

124. (a)   **(i)** 16.67%

        (ii) Any two from – measures the success in selling goods; shows the gross profit earned per $100 of sales, can be compared with previous years, can be compared with other businesses, shows that approximately 83% of the sales income is spent on the cost of goods.

    (b)   **(i)** 11.90%

        (ii) Any two from – measures the overall success of the business, shows the net profit earned per $100 of sales, can be compared with previous years, can be compared with other businesses, shows that approximately 5% of the sales income on expenses.

    (c)   **(i)** 15.00%

        (ii) Any two from – shows the profit earned per $100 of capital employed, can be compared with previous years, can be compared with other businesses, measures the profitability of the investment in the business, shows how efficiently the capital is being employed.

    (d)   **(i)** 16.8 times

        (ii) Two from – reduce inventory levels, generate more sales activity, only replace inventory when needed

Chapter 24

126. (a)   A payslip provides an employee with details of gross pay, statutory deductions, voluntary deductions, cumulative figures for gross pay, statutory deductions and voluntary deductions.

    (b)   A time sheet is completed by an employee to show the hours worked each day and is often used when the employee works away from the premises. A clock card is inserted into a time recording device (often located just inside the factory door) when the employee enters and leaves the premises; this provides a record of the hours worked.

    (c)   Leena $242: Fatima $266.60

127. (a)   Salim $190: Salman $160 (minimum wage)

    (b)   Time basis is when employees are paid an agreed amount for each hour worked. Piece rate basis is when employees are paid an agreed amount for each article produced or each task performed.

122 *Cambridge O Level Principles of Accounts Workbook*

128. (a) $306 **(b)** $242.20

129. Debit wages $1875, credit cash $1875: debit wages $425, credit income tax $140, national insurance $220, pension contributions $52, trade union subscriptions $13: debit national insurance $580, national insurance $875, pension contributions $210, trade union subscriptions $65, credit bank $1730

Chapter 25

131. Explanation of any four from – payroll, inventory records, sales ledger and invoicing and credit control, purchases ledger.

133. Accountants work with generally accepted rules such as accounting principles (e.g. prudence and consistency) and standards. Preparing financial statements for the temporary benefit of one individual is against these rules. Accountants are expected by the profession and by the public to produce reliable financial information. An accountant could be penalised for not following agreed practice.

134. Present situation – Janice is applying the minimum legal requirements regarding the health and safety of the workforce and the general public. She has a moral duty to consider whether the present precautions are adequate and whether additional measures would greatly improve the safety of the workforce and the general public. The tasks performed and the diligence and reliability of the workforce may morally justify a higher rate of pay.

Possible future situation – Janice should consider other factors in addition to profit. The safety of these products should be considered (both from the point of view of the workforce and the customers). The results of clinical tests and trials should be required (and whether any testing on animals was carried out). Janice should consider the effects on the reputation of her business, the effects of redundancies, the effects on the local population etc.